DATE DUE

Demco, Inc. 38-293

BACKCOUNTRY SNOWBOARDING

Christopher Van Tilburg

THE
MOUNTAINEERS

rs

M 1001 SW Klickitat Way, Suite 201
Seattle, WA 98134

©1998 by Christopher Van Tilburg

First edition, 1998

Published simultaneously in Great Britain by Cordee, 3a DeMontfort Street, Leicester, England, LE1 7HD

Manufactured in the United States of America

Edited by Deborah Kaufmann
All photographs ©1998 Christopher Van Tilburg, except as noted
Illustrations by Scott Gaudette
Layout by Jennifer Shontz
Snowboards design by Jennifer Shontz and Kristy L. Welch

In an effort to avoid product endorsement, the snowboard graphics designed for this book use fictional brand names that reflect the spirit of snowboarding culture.

The author of this book has attempted to educate snowboarders through commenting on various products. All opinions stated are those of the author. Neither this publication nor its contents have been prepared, approved, or licensed by any of the companies whose names or products are mentioned herein.

Cover photograph: *Big Air in Utah's Wasatch Range,* ©1998 James W. Kay
Frontispiece: *Snowshoeing up Mill D North Fork, Big Cottonwood Canyon, Utah*

Library of Congress Cataloging-in-Publication Data

Van Tilburg, Christopher.
    Backcountry snowboarding / Christopher Van Tilburg. — 1st ed.
        p.   cm.
    Includes bibliographical references (p.   ) and index.
    ISBN 0-89886-578-6
    1. Snowboarding. I. Title.
  GV857.S57V36 1998
  796.9—dc21
                                           9818828
                                           CIP

for Jennifer

CONTENTS

Splitboarding above timberline, Cooper Spur, Mount Hood, Oregon

ACKNOWLEDGMENTS

My parents, Wayne and Eleanor Van Tilburg, supported me from the beginning in myriad ways.

My colleagues and friends—fellow writers, health care professionals, snowboarders, and mountaineers—helped with manuscript development in various stages. For their critical advice I am deeply indebted. They include Stephen Bezruchka, M.D.; Scott Carr; Dan Carter, M.D.; Jon Ciambotti, M.D.; Colin Grissom, M.D.; Michael Koster; Tim Phillips, M.D.; Geoff Richardson, M.D.; Ivan Rokos, M.D.; Tom Routh; Matt Ryan, R.N.; and Peter Van Tilburg. Tom Kimbourough, Evelyn Lees, and Bruce Tremper of the Utah Avalanche Forecast Center added valuable input.

Thanks to DaKine, Gregory Packs, Duotone Snowboards, Rossignol Snowboards, Cirqueworks Packs, K2 Snowboards, Leki Poles, Life-Link, Tubbs Snowshoes, Voilé Equipment, and Winterstick Snowboards for helping with gear.

Special thanks go to friends Jim and Susie Kay for providing adventure and additional photographs.

I am proud to be part of The Mountaineers Books. Margaret Foster believed in this project from the beginning. Many thanks to the entire crew, especially Cindy Bohn, Helen Cherullo, Deborah Kauffman, Emily Kerr, Janet Kimball, Alison Koop, Uma Kukathas, Alice Merrill, Jennifer Shontz, and Kristy Welch.

Thanks to Scott Gaudette for illustrations.

Most of all, I thank my partner in life, Jennifer Wilson.

INTRODUCTION: FIRST TRACKS

Storms begin out at sea, sucking up moisture from the vast oceans. Stealthily and ominously, these storms move inland. Big clouds whirl, billow, and cool when they hit the mountains. Moisture condenses and snow falls. White and pure, the snow drifts down to settle on the mountainsides. For a brief moment in the hydrologic cycle, we can play and rejoice in the snow.

Snow. Chills travel through our nerves and our adrenaline begins to boil. Like a magnet, the mountain draws us. Driven by an automatic and uncontrollable urge, we drop everything and head to the hills. We float through light, dry powder: deep and steep. We climb a peak and carve through the snow in warm sun: smooth and fast.

We ride with our buddies in the wild backcountry, far from crowds, phones, and faxes, work and school, smog, traffic, and buildings. The backcountry is a magical, spiritual place, a natural world of solace and beauty.

WHY DO WE RIDE?

The answer seems obvious but some people may still ask, "Why backcountry snowboarding?" For ages mountaineers have had difficulty explaining their desire to climb mountains. For some, the peace and serenity of the backcountry is enough to lure us away from crowded resorts. The wonder and beauty of the natural world are unparalleled compared to mechanical lifts and machine-groomed runs. For others, the reward of hiking to earn the ride down is the ticket for thrill. The challenge of negotiating the variable snow and terrain of the winter and mountain wilderness cannot be matched in developed resorts.

Sooner or later many of us head to the backcountry for the ride of all rides: snowboarding.

WHAT IS BACKCOUNTRY SNOWBOARDING?

The next question you may be asked is a bit easier to answer: "What is backcountry snowboarding?" Backcountry snowboarding, by its simplest definition, is riding outside the boundaries or operating hours of a developed mountain resort. A backcountry snowboarding tour may entail a short, one-day hike near home or a multiday alpine climb in a foreign country. The backcountry is not always remote land, and may include popular recreation areas, public parks, and even hills near towns and roads.

Backcountry snowboarding also includes hiking out of bounds of winter resorts and riding in the resort area before and after the season. In addition, backcountry snowboarding may require helicopter and snowcat tours, which involve the utilization—and the benefit—of a ride up and the support of a professional mountain guide.

Backcountry snowboarding is a year-round, all-season sport. Late fall through midspring is the snow season in the Northern Hemisphere. In the high country, alpine climbing and snowboarding continue well into summer. And a few lucky souls head to New Zealand or South America for riding in the off-season.

On the extreme end, backcountry snowboarding can include technical alpine climbing. *Snowboard mountaineering* usually refers to climbing a peak and then riding it down. Big mountains like Rainier, Denali, the Himalayas, and Andes have all been climbed and snowboarded.

WHY THIS BOOK?

This book came about for two main reasons. First, as backcountry snowboarding and backcountry winter sports in general are becoming more popular, the need to educate riders is becoming increasingly important. This book was designed to help snowboarders understand and use the skills and equipment necessary for the sport as well as the fundamental methods for traveling in the mountains. The book also focuses on helping everyone ride safely. Wherever you go, the backcountry is wildly different from winter resorts. At resorts, professional avalanche control, ski patrol, and heated lodges dramatically decrease the risk of environmental hazards such as frostbite, hypothermia, and avalanche. Logged runs, snow-grooming machines, and the daily presence of hundreds of skiers and snowboarders radically alter the terrain as well.

Second, the mechanics of snowboarding are quite different from other types of winter sports, especially backcountry skiing. For example, having both feet attached to one board with a relatively large surface area allows us to fly through deep powder with ease. However, because of these same mechanics, we cannot advance uphill or across flat terrain, and the risk of danger from avalanche is increased.

This book was written to educate snowboarders, both because more of us are heading to the back of beyond and because much of the instructional material out there is for skiers or general mountaineers.

Keep in mind that this book is for everyone. It's for hard-core riders, cross-over skiers, and advanced resort riders searching for good snow; for snowboarders who already enjoy the backcountry but need to broaden their skills; and for backcountry skiers and mountaineers looking for a new ride. Some snowboarders are also skiers, especially those of us who formerly used short skis for hiking and now use split boards. We are snowshoers, climbers, and hikers, too. Young and old, this book is for anyone stoked for backcountry snowboarding.

HOW TO USE THIS BOOK

Chapter One offers a broad introduction to backcountry snowboarding, snowboarding history, and the mountain environment. The history of snowboarding helps us understand our roots and gives some insight into the future of the sport. The important differences among snowboards in the backcountry are also highlighted. Wilderness issues such as access, ethics, and responsibility are discussed in this chapter as well. You may have heard this information before, but if you are new to the backcountry, the health of the ecosystem and the safety of your ride depend on your staying abreast of these issues.

Chapter Two covers equipment. If you are just getting interested in the backcountry, this is an important chapter to read before you start searching for gear. If you are well versed in backcountry skiing and mountaineering but want to start snowboarding, this chapter will be helpful to you as well. You always want to use good equipment in excellent working condition. Try to buy the best gear you can afford, as some safety equipment may save your life.

Chapter Three presents a broad background in mountain and winter travel, covering such topics as foul weather, hazardous terrain, and dangerous snow conditions. You will need to know about weather reading, routefinding, general mountain safety, and survival. But reading about mountain safety and buying the gear is not enough. Take a course on general mountaineering or backcountry winter travel from a reputable source. You will see a recurring triad of terms in this text relating to safety: instruction, practice, and experience, all of which are necessary for longterm safety in the mountains.

In addition to mountain safety, Chapter Four is devoted entirely to avalanche safety because this topic is so important. Again, supplement this information by taking a class. Many areas now have avalanche safety seminars given by snowboarders for snowboarders.

Chapter Five deals with my specialty: first aid. Hopefully you will stay in shape and always ride safely. But accidents do happen in the backcountry. If you know what to do in an emergency, your knowledge can change a potentially dangerous situation into an organized rescue effort. Again, you should understand basic first-aid and self-rescue techniques by supplementing this chapter with a mountaineering-oriented first-aid course.

Chapter Six is geared toward learning approach and ascent. Because of the nature of snowboarding, you will need to be proficient at snowshoeing, free-heel skiing, or alpine climbing, depending on your preferred mode of ascent and the characteristics of the terrain. In other words, you need to climb before you ride. In particular, split boards, the newest tool with which to access the backcountry, are discussed.

Chapter Seven offers material on the really fun part: riding the backcountry.

This chapter covers it all—from powder to corn and from steeps to air. Keep in mind that you should venture into the backcountry only when you are an advanced snowboarder. You should feel comfortable with the variable terrain and snow conditions found in the backcountry. Basically, you should be able to ride any black diamond slope at a developed mountain resort, in any snow and weather conditions.

TERMINOLOGY

If you are new to the backcountry or snowboarding, some of the terminology may be new as well. The vernacular is important to know in order to communicate with and learn from others, whether they are snowboarders, skiers, rangers, or your riding pals. Many terms are defined both in the text and glossary. For example, the latest buzzword in popular literature is *glisse*. Derived from the French glisser, to slide, this term refers to all edged snow tools: telemark, alpine, and alpine touring skis as well as snowboards.

For the most part, slang has been omitted. A few terms, most borrowed from skateboard or surfing lingo, are so descriptive and particular to snowboarding that they are included.

A NOTE ABOUT SAFETY

Safety is an important concern in all outdoor activities. No book can alert you to every hazard or anticipate the limitations of every reader. The descriptions of techniques in this book are intended to provide general information. This is not a complete text on mountaineering, avalanche safety, or snowboarding technique. Nothing substitutes for formal instruction, routine practice, and plenty of experience. When you follow any of the procedures described here, you assume responsibility for your own safety. Use *Backcountry Snowboarding* as a general guide to further information. What will be covered are the basics so you can get an idea of skills needed and supplement them accordingly. The appendix lists additional resources, including books that cover nearly every chapter, as well as magazines, internet sites, and local sources. Learning about backcountry snowboarding is an ongoing process that commences with this book—and hopefully never ends.

Following pages: Hellgate, Wasatch Range, Utah ©James Kay

CHAPTER ONE

BEGINNINGS

EARLY DAYS

Snow skiing began as a method of transportation in Scandinavia some five thousand years ago, and sledding of various forms has probably been around as long. Since the 1920s, snowboard-like sleds have been reportedly used as a form of recreation in France. The first commercial breakthrough was in 1965 when Sherman Poppen of Michigan invented the Snurfer. Poppen, an engineer, saw his daughter in his backyard riding one ski, standing up. He built the prototype in his garage by screwing two skis together. The Snurfer was born as a plywood, stand-up sled with a nose leash that had similar dimensions to those of a water ski.

The Snurfer was marketed by Brunswick Company and enjoyed success in the 1960s and early 1970s. Poppen sold half a million Snurfers in the early days. Snurfer contests were even held, through the 1970s.

Sherman Poppen's classic Snurfer

Early Wintersticks prototypes, Dimitrije Milovich design

Influenced by skiing and surfing, engineer Dimitrije Milovich of Salt Lake City began designing snowboards in 1969. In the early 1970s, Milovich was granted a patent for Winterstick and began selling the boards worldwide. The early shapes were designed for and tested in the legendary deep powder of Little Cottonwood Canyon in the Wasatch Range in Utah. The laminated wood board was as long as a snow ski and three times as wide. The early boards, like the Snurfers, had no bindings. Winterstick riders initially hiked up wearing boots in the deep powder until they realized they could hike faster and farther with snowshoes.

Two early Snurfer riders are credited with making enormous contributions to snowboarding. Jake Burton of Vermont began modifying Snurfers in the 1960s and later started Burton Snowboards. Skateboarder Tom Sims of California began building his own boards in the 1960s as well, and went on to start Sims Snowboards. Both companies are still in production today.

In the 1970s, the sport of snowboarding blossomed. Along with the early work of Milovich, Burton, and Sims, others made major contributions. Bob Weber designed a ski board and eventually helped Sims build one of his first production models. Chuck Barfoot used new materials like fiberglass to design boards with Sims, and later began

16

his own company. Jeff Grell developed the high-back binding. Mike Olson started Gnu Snowboards, and Chris Sanders, Avalanche Snowboards.

A number of milestones helped propel snowboarding into the mainstream. In 1977, Milovich confirmed that snowboards were covered under ski liability insurance, thus giving them credibility at the resorts and setting up the boom of the 1980s. In 1978, Burton was the first to ride a Burton board with bindings in a Snurfer contest.

Later, snowboard contests sprang up, as did hundreds of companies. Designers went through major changes every year. Boots, bindings, and boards evolved, using the technology of a well-advanced ski industry and the ideas of surfers and skateboarders. Now, beginning with the 1998 Nagano games, snowboarding is an Olympic sport.

SNOWBOARDING TODAY

Snowboarding is one of the fastest growing winter sports. It has separated into three general disciplines, mostly geared to winter resorts: free riding, freestyle, and alpine.

Free riding is what most of us do: ride a wide variety of snow and terrain. Also called all-mountain snowboarding, free riding uses a board that is versatile for all types of snow and terrain conditions. *Soft boots* are a specialized version of pack boots, with stiff rubber soles and firm, lace-up leathers or synthetic uppers. *High-back bindings,* sometimes called soft or strap bindings, are plastic, with two or three straps for the foot. *Step-in boots and bindings*, the newest technology, are now available for soft boots, and are preferred by many resort riders. A plate mounted in the sole of the boot mates with a plate in the board. This does not spontaneously release in the manner of an alpine ski, but allows the binding to quickly detach, usually by moving a lever.

Freestyle snowboarding focuses on aerial maneuvers and tricks. Freestyle boards are usually smaller than free-riding boards to allow for quick turns. They have a soft flex and a symmetric shape from tip to tail. Boots and bindings are more flexible than those designed for free riding.

Alpine riding and racing focuses on carving turns. Length and stiff flex make these boards stable at high speeds and permit fast, tight turns. *Hard boots* are made of plastic similar to downhill ski boots, and *plate bindings,* with a heel bail and toe clip, are similar to those used for step-in crampons or alpine touring.

SNOWBOARDS IN THE BACKCOUNTRY

The Backcountry Today

In the early days, snowboarding was truly a backcountry sport before it was accepted by the ski resorts and blossomed into mainstream winter recreation. Early boards like the Snurfer, Burton Backhill, and Winterstick Swallowtail were born and bred in the backcountry. But just as technology has permeated nearly every other aspect of our lives, so too has it affected snowboarding, which has surged into the high-tech sports arena. We have speciality backcountry snowboard gear, electronic avalanche beacons, and sophisticated weather instruments to help our ride.

Backcountry snowboarding is most similar to free riding. In fact, many of us used our free-riding resort board and boots, coupled with snowshoes and hiking poles, as our first backcountry gear. Yet, backcountry snowboarding borrows heavily from all three disciplines mentioned earlier. Borrowed from alpine riding, narrow boards, stiff boots, and high-angled stances are utilized by extreme riders, for whom tight turns and edge control are crucial. Taken from freestyle are the wide stances, flexible boards, and soft boots that are favored by those who ride deep powder.

However, the variable terrain and snow conditions of the backcountry necessitate special skills and tools. Equipment specifically designed for backcountry snowboarding, such as snowshoes, backpacks, clothing, avalanche safety gear, hiking poles, and crampons, is becoming widely available. Backcountry snowboards and boots are, likewise, now a part of the product line for most major snowboard companies.

Snowboards were quickly found to excel in the backcountry from the early days. One main reason is that snowboarders have both feet fixed to one board with a large surface area. Thus, snowboards are well supported on the snowpack. In deep powder, snowboards float well, and in heavy, wet crud they ride on top instead of sinking in.

But to be efficient and well versed in backcountry snowboarding—steeps, deep powder, technical terrain, jumps—you need to gain experience in a wide variety of snowboarding techniques and styles. Free riding, freestyle, and alpine techniques and equipment all have a place in the backcountry, as you will read in later chapters.

Safety Issues

With the advent of backcountry snowboarding came some new problems and the reemergence of some old issues. These problems are described later in detail, but a brief synopsis of special circumstances regarding snowboards in the backcountry will help highlight why this type of snowboarding is different and why safety is such an important issue.

Routefinding. Snowboarders ride with a sideways stance, use bindings that do not spontaneously release in most cases, and have both feet fixed to a single board. Thus you cannot go uphill or across flat terrain on a snowboard, and must hike. Hiking uses lots of energy, slows travel, and possibly prolongs exposure to dangerous situations. Therefore, routefinding for snowboarders is quite different from routefinding for skiers.

Avalanches. In the event of an environmental hazard, especially an avalanche, snowboarders may fare worse than skiers. Due to the large area of a snowboard, if a snowboarder is caught in an avalanche, he or she is likely to be sucked down. Skiers are advised to kick off their skis when in a slide, which is nearly impossible for snowboarders to do. Also, past experience has shown that skiers able to easily remove skis after being partly buried are also able to dig themselves out faster.

Deep snow and tree wells. A similar dilemma for snowboarders is deep snow immersion. Snowboarders, skiers, and mountaineers have all fallen headfirst into deep snow or tree wells, the area under a tree where snow does not accumulate as much, thus leaving a deep hole in the snow around the tree. Victims unable to right themselves have died by suffocation, as thick snow does not allow air to penetrate. Snowboarders may fare worse than skiers in this situation, as they unable to easily detach from a board upon which both feet are fixed.

Technical terrain. Because the snowboarder has a sideways stance on a single, shorter edge, a snowboard reacts differently than do skis, especially on a steep, narrow, icy chute. Also, with the sideways stance, the rider experiences a blind spot when turning. Riders are either *regular foot,* which means they ride with left foot forward, or *goofy foot* and ride with right foot forward.

Keep these issues in mind as you read through subsequent chapters. Snowboards respond differently in certain situations and it is important to accommodate them in regard to safety.

THE BACKCOUNTRY ENVIRONMENT

Before heading into the backcountry, the snowboarder needs to address a few issues concerning access, ethics, and the environment. The overriding message is: help us save our riding terrain and the environment. You may have heard this before but the issue is important enough to read about again. The wildlands have been here longer than snowboarding or humans, and will last well beyond our lives on earth.

Access

As defined earlier, the backcountry includes a wide variety of public and private lands. Access poses particular problems, especially regarding winter resorts and public land.

Winter resorts. First, a distinction needs to be made about backcountry access from ski areas. If you buy a ticket for a lift or ride in an area controlled by a winter resort, you have to follow the rules and regulations of that resort. This even applies if you buy a one-ride lift ticket and then legally hike out-of-bounds.

Some resorts have areas they call backcountry even though the land in question is still within the boundary owned or leased by the resort. These buffer zones are controlled similarly to the rest of the resort, and include ski patrol and avalanche control. You are permitted to enter these areas only if they are open.

Heading out of bounds to search for untracked, Mount Millicent, Utah

Control gate warning signs, Brighton backcountry, Utah

Other ski areas have access gates to the true backcountry that allow you to ride the lift and then hike out-of-bounds at your own risk in uncontrolled, unpatrolled areas. You should learn the distinction between closed backcountry areas within ski area boundaries and true backcountry accessed via a gate. Some resorts do not allow any out-of-bounds riding. Check with the ski patrol at the resort if you are unsure of the regulations.

Public and private land. In public backcountry areas, local, state, and federal agencies have jurisdiction and you should follow the appropriate rules and regulations. For example, in the United States, each state's department of transportation or county sheriff controls roads, whereas the U.S. Forest Service, National Park Service, or Bureau of Land Management governs most backcountry areas on federal land. You will need to respect private property or private companies that have leases on public land, such as timber and mining concerns.

When in doubt, check with a local agency, snowboard or backcountry shop, or ski patrol. Befriend local rangers, ski patrollers, and others who enforce rules and regulations. Not only can they help you out of a jam if necessary, but most likely they can direct you to the best runs and snow.

Low-impact Backcountry Travel

Low-impact backcountry travel is of utmost importance because mountain eco-systems are so fragile. Each of us, whether a snowboarder or other type of mountaineer, must preserve and protect the natural world. After all, we are merely visitors, passing through the home of plants and animals.

Trails. Trails make one of the largest impacts on the terrain, especially dirt approach trails. Always stay on the trail and hike in single file. This helps to avoid the trampling of fragile plants, especially in early or late seasons. Also, hiking off trails, especially making shortcuts between switchbacks, can lead to erosion. Stay on the snow as much as possible.

If you need to mark trails, use *wands,* thin bamboo poles topped with bright flags, or *cairns,* small stacks of rocks. Remove trail markers upon descent. If you are on a designated trail that is maintained by an agency, do not remove already existing trail markers. Usually these markers are there to help keep people on route and to lessen damage to the surrounding area.

Roads. Like trails, roads greatly damage the ecosystem. Stay on roads and do not make your own. Park in designated parking areas.

Plants and animals. Try to leave the flora and fauna in its natural state, undisturbed as much as possible. Do not pick flowers or take rocks. Respect animals and their dens from a distance. With a few exceptions, most animals will not attack or bother humans unless they are threatened in some way, as when their nests, dens, or territory are invaded and when they protect themselves or their young in defense.

Personal waste. Pack out all your garbage and manage your human waste correctly. Some areas that are frequented, like Denali and Mount Rainier, have a human waste problem. In the cold mountain environment human waste does not decompose quickly. This is especially important to remember when climbers need to melt snow for drinking water. Be aware of regulations in watershed areas and use the portable toilets in the parking area or at campsites. Some high camps on snow have latrines. If not, bury stool several hundred yards away from water in a shallow dirt hole, or smear it on a rock so that it will decompose more rapidly. Pack out your toilet paper, also.

Remember that the old mountaineering axioms hold as true for snowboarders as everyone else on the mountains: "Take nothing but pictures, leave nothing but footprints" and "Pack it in, pack it out."

Camping. If you are camping, chose a campsite at least two hundred feet away from streams and off fragile plants. Use designated campsites whenever possible. Do not make wind blocks from rocks; use a tent or build a snow shelter instead. Store food in trees out of reach of animals.

Fires. Cook and melt drinking water with a small camp stove. Avoid building a fire just for pleasure. Make a fire only when you really need to dry out gear, get warm, or cook when you are low on fuel. If you do start a fire, keep it small by burning small, downed sticks no thicker than your wrist. Make sure you douse

On the trail to a late summer bonus run, Cooper Spur, Mount Hood, Oregon

the fire with water or snow, scatter cold, wet ashes, and remove the fire ring.

Pets. Avoid bringing pets into the wilderness. This is especially important in watershed areas to prevent contamination of the water supply.

Mountain Courtesy

In addition to low-impact travel, we all should observe basic mountain courtesy so that everyone can share the wonders of the wilds and keep the snow in good condition long into the season. Some generally accepted guidelines are well known to backcountry users.

On trail. Watch for others. Be careful not to put your party or others at risk by following too closely behind or climbing above someone else. Hike and talk quietly. Do not stop on the trail. Step aside to let faster parties pass. Share safety information with passing parties. Help others when they are in need of guidance or assistance.

It is permissible to use an existing ski track up a popular backcountry slope if you are on short skis or a split board, but not on snowshoes. Hikers should break a separate trail since boot and snowshoe tracks can render the ski trail useless for future ascents via skis or split boards.

Riding. If you are atop a backcountry run with another group, the first group up should have first tracks down. Ride slopes one person at a time. Ride in control and be able to stop in an instant. If you fall, fill in the depression by scooping snow into the hole and packing it down.

When riding, keep your track next to the trees or alongside another's track. Try not to cut up the entire run. Keep in mind that skiers and snowboarders view the mountain differently. A snowboarder may want to bank off a cornice whereas a skier might head down the fall line. Lay tracks to take some powder for yourself but leave as much fresh snow as possible for others. The snow may be so good that you will want to hike up for another run.

If you are riding spring corn, try not to stay too late in the day. Snowboards can cruise through afternoon slush but will leave heavy ruts and ruin the snow for the next day (see Chapter Six).

LEARNING

I still remember my first day on skis. My dad held me under my armpits and my skis tracked between his on three inches of gooey snow over frozen grass and manure. I was skiing down the cow pasture behind our house on a wet, gray Pacific Northwest day. Back then, if you wanted to ride in the snow, you pretty much had to ride skis.

I can also clearly remember the pain of my first day riding a snowboard years later. The headache. The soreness in my knees and butt. The whiplash to my neck with every fall on my backside. My gloves were sopping wet. My wrist and ankles were fatigued. By the second run my entire body was throbbing with pain and soaking wet.

I first rode a Burton Backhill on Mount Hood in Oregon. The sideways stance and soft boots felt strange. The flimsy straps bound my feet to the board. The board itself was a short piece of plywood with an upturned nose. It had no metal edges but two aluminum fins were attached to a dovetail.

I spent most of the time on my backside. I would alternately hit my butt, then whiplash my head with a loud thud that left me with a ripping headache. Every time I fell, I took longer to get up. The next time I went snowboarding, I wore knee pads and stuffed two hats in my pants to pad my behind. I made more turns and fell less.

Many years later I summited and rode Mount Hood during the month before I got married. Snowboarding had long since metamorphosed into a refined snow sport and the sideways stance had become, for me, a natural, preferred feeling. But every time I head up Hood or see an old Burton Backhill on the wall of a shop, I remember the early days. The humbling agony of being a beginner. The days I wanted to quit but forced myself to call a learning experience. The pain of pounding the ground hard.

The more time you spend in the backcountry, the sharper the feel you will get for common courtesy, especially regarding rules that apply to particular sites. If you do not know, ask. If someone asks you, educate them.

Responsibility

As mountaineers, we know to always exercise responsibility and self-reliance. Both of these characteristics are gained with instruction, practice, and experience in the mountain and winter environments, as previously noted.

Always use good judgment based on your own knowledge and skills. Be physically and mentally prepared. Stay within your skill level. Alter your plans and abort a tour if conditions do not look good, no matter how far you are into the trip. Remember it is up to you to evaluate avalanche and weather conditions, the condition of the route, and the gear you will need.

Rescue is never immediate nor automatic. Try to take care of yourself and your party when in trouble but do not be afraid to ask for help early. Similarly, any help you can give to others in need will be greatly appreciated by skiers and snowboarders alike.

Be Proactive

We all love the backcountry and are willing to put in hours of work gathering our gear, planning our route, and making the trek to the top. But the natural world is a special place and does not take well to pollution, development, and civilization. Get involved to help save the environment.

Try to car pool or ride the bus to the mountains. Do your best to reduce, reuse, and recycle to conserve use of products that come from the mountains. If you can, attend fund-raisers, lectures, and meetings having to do with the health of the mountains.

Consider getting involved with a local or national group that protects the mountain environment, such as the Snowrider Program of Surfrider Foundation. Started as an environmental foundation to keep the ocean and surf beaches clean, Surfrider Foundation recognized the link between surfing and snowboarding: their mutual use of the hydrologic cycle. The hydrologic cycle starts out at sea as moisture evaporates. Clouds move inland, and snow falls in the mountains. The snow melts to runoff that is drained by streams back to the ocean to start the cycle again. The Snowrider Program educates snowboarders about the health of the water cycle, including the protection, preservation, and restoration of the environment.

The trail home, North Sister, Oregon

CHAPTER TWO

EQUIPMENT

For many of us, our first backcountry experience was hiking up a boot trail near a ski area and riding the all-mountain board we used at resorts. But the more you ride in the backcountry, the more you need gear designed specifically for rugged conditions.

The wide variety of snowboarding and mountaineering gear can be confusing, but you may have some of it already. Check with experts at your local shop for more information and to get your gear properly fitted. Try to get the best equipment you can afford.

SNOWBOARDS

Snowboards are highly technical and significantly variable in shape and construction. With so many companies making boards nowadays, which board to buy can be a tough decision. In general, backcountry snowboards are similar to free-riding or all-mountain designs, with features that help negotiate them in the different snow and terrain of the backcountry. Many backcountry boards are also labeled as extreme, big mountain, or long boards.

Because of the wide variety of terrain and snow in all parts of the world, choose a board that suits your area and the type of riding you most often do. Most riders find that two or three boards make an excellent collection, or quiver, for nearly all backcountry conditions. If you can only afford one board, stay with something basic. The most important factors regarding shape are length, width, side cut, nose and tail scoop, and flex. When looking at these factors, keep in mind that most trade off between flotation and maneuverability.

Length

Do not buy a board by length alone. The overall shape affects the way the board handles. Use length as your first guideline. Take into account your height, weight, riding style, and the type of snow and terrain in which you usually ride.

Longer boards in the 170-to-200-centimeter range are better for deep snow and wide open bowls. In powder, longer boards give more flotation, provide stability at high speeds, and make landing jumps easier. Because they are heavier and longer, they are less maneuverable in tight spots and trees.

Medium boards 160-170 centimeters long provide a blend of maneuverability in tight spots and flotation in deep snow. Most riders who can only buy one backcountry board choose one of medium length.

Shorter boards ranging from 145 to 160 centimeters are

Snowboard dimensions

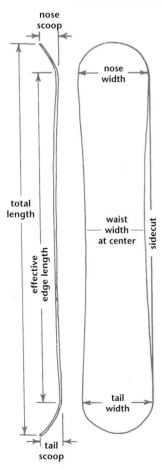

better for technical terrain and areas with trees. They allow for good control and tight turns. Short boards are also lighter, something to consider when you are going to be carrying one on alpine climbs or long approaches.

Width

Most boards have their width measured at the nose, waist, and tail. When considering waist width, most boards measure around twenty-five centimeters. Wider boards increase the surface area and give more flotation in powder. Some wide boards are specifically designed for people with large feet so that their toes and heels do not drag over the edge. Narrow boards are usually coupled with a deeper side cut (explained below). They allow for tighter turns on more technical terrain.

Side Cut

Side cut, measured in a radius, is the arc in the side of the board. It mainly affects edge control and turning. A deeper side cut, or smaller radius of about 800-900 centimeters, helps you to carve tighter, quicker turns. A shallow side cut, or larger radius of around 1,000 centimeters, is designed for bigger turns and speed.

Nose and Tail Scoop

Most backcountry boards have *directional shape,* meaning the tip and tail have different characteristics. One difference is in the *scoop,* the degree of upturn in the nose and tail. A significant nose scoop is important when in deep snow, to prevent the nose from diving. Tail scoop, also important, allows you to ride backward as needed in some situations.

The nose and tail scoop also affect the amount of edge that is in contact with the snow, the *effective edge.* When you check the length of the board, compare the overall length with the effective edge length. The more nose and tail scoop, the shorter the effective edge when compared to the overall length. In general, a longer effective edge gives you more contact with the slope, and therefore is more stable, especially when on steep or icy slopes. But the greater the nose scoop, the easier it is to keep the board floating in deep snow.

If you ride more technical terrain in hard snow, effective edge is more important; if you ride mostly powder, the nose scoop will make more of a difference.

Flex

Flex describes the degree of pliability of the board. In general, a softer flex is more forgiving and allows for increased maneuverability, as when riding powder. *Camber* is the amount of preshaped flex that is built into the board. A stiffer board is more difficult to turn but lends stability, especially on technical terrain. Most boards are directional with regard to flex, as they are with shape. Often the tail is stiffer to give control and the nose is softer for easier maneuverability.

Big swallowtail for deep powder, legendary Wasatch backcountry, Utah

Construction

Like shape, construction influences performance. Without going into too much detail, here are the basics. Boards are usually fabricated with *laminated construction* or *cap construction*. Laminated boards, in which the materials are layered and a separate sidewall makes up the edges, are easy to repair. They are durable but often heavier. Cap construction, in which the top sheet is wrapped around the edge, eliminating the need for a separate sidewall, is generally lighter and more responsive. A variety of construction combinations is available as well.

A board's core material is usually wood or foam, with fiberglass and other composite material used for laminating. Wood cores are more common as they are firm, responsive, and durable. Less popular foam cores are softer and thus more flexible. They are less responsive but dampen vibrations better than wood.

Board bases are usually made from polyethylene, using one of two techniques. *Sintered* bases, those formed by heating powdered polymers, are faster, hold wax well, and are durable. *Extruded* bases, made by forcing polymer through a die, are less expensive and easier to repair.

Swallowtails

Swallowtails are not simply long boards, but lean, sleek powder guns akin to big wave surfboards. They are specialized boards, designed for deep powder, nothing else. Swallowtails range from 170 to 200 centimeters in length. The long length and wide nose allow them to plane early in deep snow. The *swallowtail*, a cutout section of the tail, decreases surface area and increases flexibility of the tail. Foregoing the spring derived from a standard tail provides maneuverability and permits deep high-speed turns. This ability to dig in and hold on to big turns is what's so magical about these boards, giving you a fast, fluid ride.

One of Winterstick's original shapes was a swallowtail influenced by swallowtail surfboards. Early Burton and Sims boards had small notches in the tails forming mini swallowtails, also called dovetails. In fact, at one time Hexell made a swallowtail ski. With the popularity of backcountry snowboarding on the rise, the swallowtail has returned. Now the snowboard companies Nitro, Winterstick, Rosignol, and A make swallowtails.

Riding a swallowtail will feel strange at first, no doubt. Do not expect to hop on one of these boards and feel like you're on an all-mountain board. Because of their length, swallowtails are solely deep-powder tools, best for wide open bowls of deep snow.

Choosing a Board

Are you thoroughly confused yet? Buying a board can be difficult, with so many different types on the market today. Start with your height, weight, and the backcountry terrain and snow conditions in which you most often ride. Also, consider whether you are buying only one board or developing a quiver.

In general, if you are heavier or taller than average, or you most often ride deep powder in wide open bowls, choose a longer board for greater flotation. If you are shorter and lighter or ride on lots of technical terrain, choose a shorter board to maximize maneuverability. Do not forget to factor in the weight of a backpack as well. Remember that it is not the length alone, but width, side cut, flex, and scoop that matter as well.

If you spend most of your days riding powder six inches deep or more, you probably want a powder board. These sticks excel on big mountains and in big snow in Alaska, Europe, New Zealand, the Rocky Mountains, the Sierras, and Canada. Consider a free-riding directional board up to ten centimeters longer than the one you ride at the resorts, with an upturned nose and medium flex. Although the effective edge is shorter and the side cut may be shallow, these factors are less important than surface area and nose scoop in powder. Some people ride a shorter board that is also wider, a combination that offers the increased maneuverability in tight spots provided by a shorter board, but still with more surface area on which to float.

If you ride on more technical terrain you may need a board with more alpine characteristics. These boards excel in spring and summer alpine climbs, in hard snow, and when riding among trees and on technical terrain. Consider a stiffer, shorter board with a deeper side cut and a longer effective edge. The deeper side cut will help you make quick turns, and the longer effective edge will provide more stability on steep slopes and hard snow.

If you can only buy one board, look for a backcountry board that has a combination of characteristics that allows you to ride on a wide variety of types of snow. For example, consider a board five to ten centimeters longer than the one you ride at resorts, to give stability at high speeds and when landing jumps. Look for a board with significant nose scoop to help you float in deep snow. Then look for a narrow waist and a deep side cut to add stability and maneuverability on steep slopes, on hard snow, or among trees.

If you are in doubt, you can often try boards at shops or on-snow demos to get a feel for them first. Ask locals about what works best in your area.

BOOTS AND BINDINGS

Now that you have your board, you need boots and bindings. With technology constantly changing, boot and binding systems can comprise the most complex and crucial link between rider and equipment. As you usually use a separate tool for approach, your boots have to be compatible with both snowboard bindings and ski, snowshoe, or crampon bindings, as discussed later.

Soft Boots and High-Back Bindings

Soft boots are comfortable and warm. They work fairly well with snowshoes when hiking. Depending on the boot, you can get a stiff or soft flex, both forward

Soft boot, mountaineering boot, hard boot   *Highback binding*

and laterally. High-back bindings fit nearly any soft boot and are adjustable in forward lean and flex. This system is responsive and permits good maneuverability and control. The high-back buckles are secure but may leave some pressure points on the top of the foot. Importantly, they are field repairable, and easily interchange for use with other boards mounted with high-back bindings. Keep in mind that most soft boots do not perform well for technical climbing, as when kicking steps into hard snow.

Step-In Boots and Bindings

Step-in bindings are relatively new. They have a plate in the boot sole that mates with a plate in the board. Unlike alpine ski bindings, they do not release spontaneously, but allow for quick release when you manually lift a lever. The boots are generally stiffer than soft boots and attach at either the toe and heel or side to side. Depending on how stiff a boot you desire, some come with external buckles and plastic support. Again, the degree of stiffness and flex varies among boot and binding systems. Bindings that connect at the toe and heel are usually more responsive edge to edge, and give lateral flex. Bindings that connect from side to side are usually less responsive edge to edge.

Step-in boots are quite easy to use and take no time to get in and out of the bindings. However, when hiking in the backcountry, snow and ice can collect on the boot and binding, making it difficult to step into the binding. The plate on the sole can also become damaged by hiking on rocks and approach trails. Also, the hardware of a high-back binding is often built into the interior of the boot. This makes field repairs difficult and limits some adjustments. No industry standard exists and you have to buy, from a single manufacturer, a boot and binding system that for the most part cannot be interchanged with others. Also, you need a good fit in order to limit the amount of play in this system.

Hard Boots and Plate Bindings

Plate bindings with hard boots give excellent edge control and are preferred by some snowboarders on technical climbs and descents, when edge control is crucial. They do not permit as much lateral flex or mobility. Plate bindings can be quickly released by moving a toe clip, and may offer some advantage in dangerous situations that necessitate getting out of your board quickly. Hard snowboard boots are not always as comfortable and can be more difficult to fit. Like step-in boots, they should fit snugly.

Plate binding

Most riders who choose hard boots use plastic boots specifically designed for backcountry riding that have flexible cuffs for hiking and rugged soles for climbing.

Other Boots

Mountaineering boots are versatile and a good compromise between hard and soft boots. They are usually double boots consisting of a lace-up foam liner and a lace-up, plastic outer shell. Mountaineering boots are becoming more popular in the backcountry because they have several advantages. They are warm, durable, and waterproof like hard snowboard boots, but more comfortable for hiking. They are compatible with both soft and hard bindings as well as with crampons, snowshoes, and some ski bindings.

Generally, mountaineering boots are not as stiff as hard snowboarding boots, so hiking is easier. As discussed later, mountaineering boots or hard snowboarding boots designed for the backcountry are essential for technical climbing.

When using mountaineering boots with high-back bindings, make sure that they fit well and that the buckles do not rub on the laces or eyelets. Mountaineering boots with plate bindings must fit well, also; the soft plastic at the toe and heel can be stressed by the toe clip and heel bail.

Another alternative to hard snowboarding boots is alpine touring ski boots. These are similar to hard snowboarding boots designed for the backcountry. These boots fit plate bindings but have features designed for the backcountry, such as lug soles for traction, cuffs that are flexible enough to hike in, and crampon-compatible soles.

Before split boards and snowshoes became so popular, a few riders even used three-pin telemark boots. The beefy plastic boots could be used with short telemark skis on the ascent and with soft snowboard bindings on the descent.

Releasable Bindings

Bindings that spontaneously release like ski bindings are now available but not widely used. The difficulty is getting both feet to simultaneously eject every time. If only one leg were to release, the huge torque of the board on the other leg could result in a disastrous injury. Some riders believe that releasable bindings are important for avalanche and deep snow burial. Others believe that the risk of only one leg releasing is too great for the benefits.

Liners and Foot Beds

A good fit to your boot is important. Most shops that sell boots have experts who can fit the boot and custom-mold the liner. Consider purchasing a foot bed that is formed to your particular foot. Customized foot beds improve fit and eliminate pressure points. You may even consider using two interchangeable inner boots. I use thick, warm inner boots for cold days and lighter-weight liners for spring and summer riding.

Stance

Probably the most controllable variable in your whole snowboarding setup is the binding stance, that is, where you mount your bindings. Binding stance is largely based on individual preference, terrain and snow conditions, and riding styles. Like boards, stance is widely variable. The following is a discussion of the basics.

Centering. Bindings are either centered over the midpoint of the board or, more commonly, one to two inches back. Riding with bindings back gives better nose control and flotation in deep snow and makes it easier to turn in steep terrain. A center-mounted or near-centered stance may offer a slight advantage when carving hard snow.

Width. Width depends on your height, board length, and type of snow in which you most often ride. A wide stance, ranging from twenty to twenty-two inches, is more stable and is usually preferred with soft snow and powder. A narrow stance, under twenty inches, gives better control for carving and is sometimes preferred with steep terrain.

Foot angle. Foot angle partly depends on the size of your feet; you do not want them hanging over the edge of the board. Flatter angles, from zero to twenty degrees, provide lots of maneuverability and stability, especially in powder. Steeper angles, ranging from twenty to forty-five degrees, are better for edge control, faster turns, and power.

Choosing a stance. Remember to try different positions and then stick with what is most comfortable and matches your

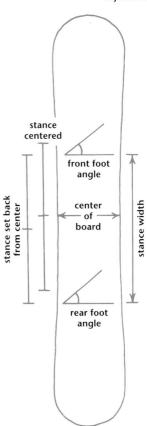

Stance adjustments

stance centered

front foot angle

stance set back from center

center of board

stance width

rear foot angle

style of riding. Some riders find they like to change stance depending on the particular board and snow and terrain conditions. Others prefer to use one stance for all boards and conditions to avoid having to reacclimatize each time they change.

Most backcountry riders start by centering their bindings one to two inches back from center, with a stance from nineteen to twenty-two inches. Many prefer a flatter back foot, from zero to fifteen degrees, and a more angled front foot, from fifteen to thirty degrees. These angles, generally steeper than resort riders use, mostly improve maneuverability and edge control. Riders who wear hard boots or ride on steep terrain may choose to have their feet angled even more.

If you use speciality boards like a swallowtail or split board you may be restricted to a particular stance. For example, long swallowtails require using a wide stance set several inches back from center. Most split boards may restrict the use of a narrow, high-angle stance.

Leash

Many bindings come with leashes and most mountain resorts require their use. The leash is designed for you to retain the board in the event that your feet come out of the bindings, a decidedly rare event if you have good equipment. In the backcountry most riders remove the leash as it offers little advantage and can be disadvantageous if you need to get out of your bindings quickly. Just do not let go of your board on the steeps or it will slide away!

TOOLS FOR APPROACH AND ASCENT

Due to the nature of snowboarding, you usually need a separate tool for ascent unless you are using a split board, as discussed below, or a vehicle such as a helicopter, snowcat, or snowmobile. Remember—your boots must be compatible with your snowboard bindings as well as whatever tool you are climbing with.

Poles

Whether you are hiking a boot trail or using a tool mentioned below, you should have poles. Poles give more stability when climbing and allow you to use your arms to improve hiking efficiency. Collapsible poles work best as they can be stowed in your pack when descending.

You can build your own collapsible poles from ski poles. Saw your pole in half. Use epoxy to glue a metal dowel into the upper section so that about one inch is in the upper pole and about one inch is left out. Drill one hole in the free end of the dowel and another in the lower section of the pole so they match up. Slide the lower section into the dowel in the upper section and use a spring clip in the aligned holes to keep both halves together.

Snowshoes

Snowshoes are easy to use and versatile. Metal-frame mountaineering snowshoes are lightweight, durable, and easily strapped to a pack when descending. On

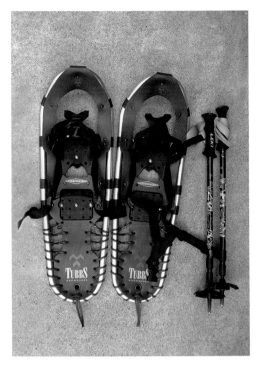

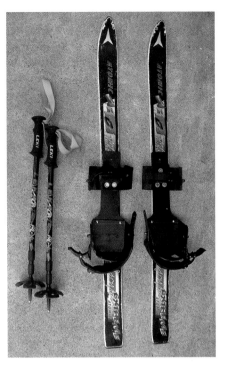

The backcountry standard: 24-inch snow-shoes and collapsible poles

A low-budget alternative: kids' skis with universal bindings

snowshoes, you can maneuver through trees and directly up slopes. Also, most snowshoe bindings are compatible with snowboard boots. However, make sure when you buy them that your boot fits in the binding. Fortunately, most bindings can be adjusted generously. *Snowshoe crampons*, spikes or traction devices on the bottom of the shoe, help improve traction.

Sizes, which are widely variable, trade off between the maneuverability of a small snowshoe and the greater flotation of a large one. The larger the pack you carry, the heavier you are, and the deeper the snow you plan to hike in, the larger the snowshoe you need. For day hikes in most areas, twenty-four-inch snowshoes work well, although on big powder days they still sink several inches. For extended overnight trips when you are carrying a heavy pack or in deep snow, you may need a longer snowshoe.

Skis

Short skis have been used in the backcountry for a long time. They offer several advantages. In many backcountry areas, you can use a ski track already put in by skiers. Or if you are touring with skiers, you can travel together instead of breaking your own snowshoe trail. Furthermore, with some long approaches, especially on firm snow or rolling hills, skis can be faster than snowshoes.

Split boards have largely replaced short skis for backcountry snowboarding. Skis are now used by people who cannot afford a split board or when a split board is undesirable, such as in technical descents when you need the integrity of a regular board but the efficiency of skis for approach.

Short skis ranging from 110 to 130 centimeters in length work best. Longer and wider skis provide more surface area for deep snow. But they need to be short enough to not drag when lashed to a pack on the way down. You can buy short skis called *firn skis*. These spring and summer mountaineering skis are short and lightweight, used when a long ski is not needed for flotation. In addition, kids' skis work excellently. They are lighter and not as durable, but since you are only using them for ascent, usually they are adequate.

Ski bindings. Bindings depend largely on what type of snowboard boots you wear. With hard snowboarding, alpine touring, or mountaineering boots, alpine touring bindings are usually used. However, these can be heavy. Some riders wear telemark boots with three-pin bindings for skiing up and soft snowboarding bindings for riding down. Even another approach is to use the lightweight *NNN boots and bindings* and carry separate snowboard boots in your pack.

Universal ski bindings are now made by Rosignol, Pika, and other companies. These hybrid bindings are similar to those used with snowshoes and snowboards, and usually have two ratchet buckles. A flexible plastic base plate mounts to the ski and the free-heel binding can be used with nearly any type of boot. These low-budget bindings are not as durable or stable as ski bindings but work well with kids' skis for lightweight climbing.

Skins. *Skins*, synthetic strips with hairs leaning in one direction like scales on a cross-country ski, are necessary for traction uphill. These directional fibers allow you to slide the ski uphill with ease, but prevent your sliding back. They attach with either a strong, reusable adhesive or straps. Because skins for short skis need to be custom-made, either cut skins to fit short skis or use long skins and wrap the excess around the tail. Also, be sure to get skins that fit the width of the ski. A *ski crampon*, a metal plate that attaches to the binding to provide additional traction, can be used as well.

If you are using synthetic skins, skin wax can be applied to provide additional holding power, especially when the skins become worn. Also, the adhesive loses its grip after a while; you can buy extra skin glue to reapply it.

Crampons and Ice Axes

On extreme terrain, such as glaciers or any other hard snow or ice on which you have difficulty hiking, skinning, or snow-shoeing, you may need *crampons*, spikes set in metal frames that attach to your boots and grip the snow.

Step-in, full-frame plate crampons are now the standard. They have a toe bail and heel clip similar to plate bindings for snowboards. You need hard snowboard or mountaineering boots that have toe and heel grooves for attachment. Lace-up crampons can be used, sometimes with modification, with soft boots, but are less desirable and reliable. K2 Snowboards has designed a crampon for step-in snowboard boots as well. Crampons come in lots of sizes and models so make sure they fit your boots properly.

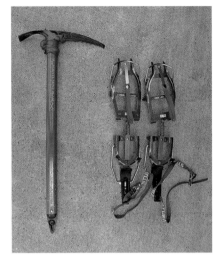

Glacier climbing tools: ice ax and crampons

If the snow is hard enough to require crampons, you will also need an *ice ax*, a tool designed to assist climbing and arrest falls on steep terrain and hard snow. When choosing an ice ax, get one that is long enough to easily reach the ground when carrying but not so long that it hits your head when lashed to your pack on descent. A shaft length of forty to fifty centimeters works for most.

Split Boards

Using a separate tool for ascent is somewhat cumbersome. Although snow-shoes, short skis, and crampons work great, you have to carry the heavy board on your back when you hike and then stash your ascent gear in your pack when riding.

Leave it to the French to solve this problem. The first experimental *split board* was reportedly made by Fanatic and called the Rando-Surf. It combines surfing-influenced snowboarding with the practicality of alpine touring, also known as *randonée*. Split a board lengthwise, detach the bindings, reattach them on the individual planks, and you have two free-heel skis for climbing.

Now well refined, these systems are available and may become the new backcountry standard for soft snow. The Nitro Tour and Voilé Split Decision are on the market. Both systems have a seam in the middle of the board and tip and tail devices to hold the halves together. When you are ready to split the board, the bindings come off and the two halves separate. Then the bindings reattach in ski fashion for climbing.

Split board: remove bindings and split two halves

Split board: (left) attach adhesive climbing skins

Split board: (right) reattach bindings and ski away (all three photos: Cooper Spur, Mount Hood, Oregon)

Split Kit. For a more economical option, Voilé has a Split Kit that you can use to convert your own board by sawing it in half. Following the instructions, you saw the board lengthwise, mount the hardware, and make your own split board, using your favorite board. There are a few disadvantages to splitting your own board. Both production models of split boards have metal edges on the inside and outside of the two halves. Thus, when you are in ski mode, you have metal edges on both sides of each ski to grip the snow. When you cut your board in half, you compromise the structural integrity of a board designed to function as a whole. The production boards are specifically designed with the split in mind.

Skins. As with short skis, skins need to be used with the split board to provide traction when climbing uphill. Nitro and Voilé make skins that are wide enough for split boards. These skins are backed with a strong adhesive that sticks well to the bottom of the board.

Skin glue may be added if the adhesive becomes worn. Skin wax also may be applied to the skin surface to increase its holding power to the snow. As with skis, crampons are available for even greater traction. Some skins come with tip and tail attachments, also.

Using a Split Board. These boards take about five minutes, if not less, to convert from ski to snowboard mode and vice versa. The huge bonuses include not having to carry the board when hiking, utilizing the efficiency of skis when climbing, and riding without the weight of snowshoes or short skis on your pack. The large surface area and wide climbing skins often make it easier to climb than when wearing snowshoes or short skis. Compared to snowshoes, split boards are often faster on long approaches, and on them you can utilize a skin track set by a party of skiers.

Split boards have seams in the middle which give more torsional flex compared to a regular board. They perform best in soft snow and powder.

If you are buying a split board or a board that you plan to cut in half and mount to make your own split board, remember that these are primarily soft-snow boards. Also, because of their design, the use of a narrow, high-angle stance is restricted and binding adjustment is somewhat limited.

MOUNTAINEERING EQUIPMENT

Snowboard gear is only a small part of equipment you need in the backcountry. You also need high-quality mountaineering gear and must know how to use it. To familiarize yourself with this equipment, it is wise to consult a mountaineering text and take a general mountaineering course. Use of the equipment is described in later chapters.

Essentials

There are certain essentials you should never be without; Table 2.1 is a composite list for snowboarders. The extra food, water, and clothing is in addition to what

TABLE 2.1: GENERAL EQUIPMENT LIST FOR BACKCOUNTRY SNOWBOARDING

ESSENTIALS

Food and water

Map, compass, altimeter

Matches, windproof and waterproof

First-aid kit

Repair materials, including duct tape, safety pin, steel wool, rubber strap, three feet of three-millimeter cord, binding screw and nut, pocket knife or tool with a #3 Phillips screwdriver

Sunglasses or goggles

Sunscreen

Headlamp with extra batteries and bulb

Water purification tablets

Extra food, water, and winter clothing

Emergency bivouac sack or plastic tarp

Snowboard backpack

Mode of ascent, such as snowshoes, skis, or split board

Cell phone (optional)

WINTER CLOTHING

Socks, wool blend

Long underwear, polypropylene

Insulating layers—two to three layers of polyester fleece, wool, or down

Parka and pants, windproof and waterproof

Hat, headband, balaclava, neck gaiter

Gauntlet gloves or mittens with fleece liners

Gaiters, supergaiters, or overboots

AVALANCHE GEAR

Avalanche transceiver, 457kHz	Snow saw
Probe or probe poles	Clinometer
Shovel	

GLACIER GEAR

Glacier	Ice ax
Crampons	Helmet
Ascenders or prusiks	Wands
Pickets, flukes, ice screws	Snow shovel and saw

Fifty to sixty meters of nine- to eleven-millimeter dynamic dry rope

Harness, belay device, carabiners, webbing, pulley

OVERNIGHT GEAR

Stove, fuel, cook pot
Sleeping bag and pad
Tent or bivouac sack
Additional food and clothing

you plan to use for your outing. Depending on the length of your tour, your first-aid and repair kits may vary. I take fewer items for day hikes than for extended trips. (See Chapter Five for recommended items.) Repair materials should include duct tape, cloth first-aid tape, steel wool, a rubber strap, a few feet of cord, a binding adjustment tool, and an extra binding screw.

Backpack. A backpack large enough to carry your gear and snowboard is also essential. For day tours, a small day pack of about fifteen hundred to two thousand cubic inches works well. It should be big enough for food, water, and extra clothes, which can be bulky. You will need a larger pack for extended climbs and overnight trips. Your packs should be durable and fit well. The shops where you buy them can fit them properly.

A basic top-loading pack can be adapted for carrying a snowboard if it has lash patches. However, the load may be unstable, and ice ax loops and the main compartment are sometimes difficult to access. Special adapters that lash onto packs, such as those from Mountainsmith or Dana Designs, can make a snowboard more stable.

A better alternative is to use a pack designed for backcountry snowboarding. These usually have front-mounted compression straps for the board, side-mounted ice ax loops, and a compartment that can easily be opened with the board strapped on. A panel-loading pack is somewhat easier to open with the board strapped on than a top-loading pack. Some panel-loading packs also have an access panel between the shoulder straps. A shovel pouch, which allows you to access your shovel quickly and store it without getting your pack wet inside, is an added bonus.

Cell phone. Whether or not to carry cell phones in the wilderness is one of the hottest debates in the mountain community. Carrying a cell phone may give you a false sense of security and prompt you to venture onto terrain or conditions you otherwise would not approach. However, if you need a rescue, a cell phone may bring faster response, which can save lives as well as minimize dangerous and costly rescues.

Winter Clothing

Synthetic clothing made from polyester is the backcountry standard. It wicks moisture well, dries quickly, retains much of its insulating properties when wet, and is lightweight and durable. Down is frequently used at high altitude and excels in cold, dry weather because it is light and easily compressed. But down does not keep you warm when wet and takes a long time to dry. Wool is heavy, especially when wet, but is warm and durable. Cotton should never be worn in the backcountry because it is a poor insulator, useless when wet, and slow to dry. This applies to briefs, bras, and long underwear since you don't want a wet layer next to your skin.

Winter clothing should consist of several layers. The under layer wicks moisture from your body. The middle one or two layers should be bulky insulation of fleece or down. The outer layer should be windproof and waterproof but permit venting of body heat. Your parka should be of good quality windproof, waterproof material. A hood, high collar, and cuffs will keep you warm. Dual front zippers and armpit zippers will help ventilate. Pants need to have side zippers for ventilatation and tight cuffs to keep the snow out.

Layering and venting are important to regulate the cold and wet outside against the body heat and sweat you generate inside. You need to stay warm and dry from the weather but also avoid overheating and getting soaked with perspiration. Use a hat, hood, neck gaiter, and headband to help regulate your body heat as well. This is important because you lose so much heat from your head. Also, carry extra clothes if you sweat a lot so you can change into a dry shirt or gloves after a long hike.

Fleece gloves or mittens with outer shells are necessary. When backcountry snowboarding, you should wear gauntlet gloves or mittens when riding to keep snow out of your cuffs. Some riders prefer mittens as they are warmer than gloves.

For socks, wool blend is the standard. Some people prefer a light sock liner and a bulky insulating sock. I wear two different boot liners depending on how cold it is and how long I am heading out, with one medium-weight sock designed for snowboarding. Depending on the conditions and how tightly your pant cuffs fit over your boots, you may need gaiters, supergaiters, or overboots as well. They add warmth and help keep snow out of your boot cuffs.

Avalanche Gear

Like the essentials, avalanche gear is something you should never be without when traveling in avalanche country. These few items can save your life but are useless without proper instruction and practice (see Chapter Four).

A *clinometer*, a protractor with a plum bob, will help you determine slope angles to identify hazardous terrain. A shovel is necessary to dig snow pits and to dig out a buried partner. Metal shovels with telescopic handles are the standard as they are large and durable. Plastic shovel blades are lightweight but less durable, especially when digging in hard snow, ice, or avalanche debris. A snow saw can make digging snow pits easier and save time.

You will need safety gear, including an *avalanche transceiver,* also called a beacon. This radio frequency broadcasts a signal when in "transmit" mode. If one person is buried, another can switch his or her beacon to "receive" mode and search for the other. The old U.S. transceiver frequency is now outdated and dual frequency transceivers are no longer available. You must carry and know how to use the new 457kHz beacon. The 457kHz single frequency is superior to dual frequency as it has a longer range and does not require earphones. Also, it is worth the extra money to buy a transceiver with both light and sound indicators to improve your searching speed. Remember: everyone in your party needs a beacon; they are useless used singly!

Also carry an avalanche probe or collapsible poles that convert to probes.

Essential avalanche gear: probe poles, shovel, probe, beacon, clinometer

Glacier Gear

In addition to crampons and an ice ax, you will need gear for alpine climbs on technical or glaciated terrain.

A helmet is important on many climbs to protect yourself from rock fall. Helmets designed for mountaineering are probably best as they are lightweight, durable, and easily adjustable should you wear a hat underneath. Snowboard helmets are available as well, but are usually designed for resort riding, when impact from a fall is more common than that from falling rock or ice.

Other mountaineering gear is designed to protect you against falling when you travel on exposed terrain, and to extricate someone from a crevasse. This gear includes a harness, rope, mechanical ascending devices or *prusiks,* which are knotted cords used for ascending rope, and other equipment like *carabiners*, the mountaineer's snap link. *Pickets, flukes,* and *ice screws* are anchors that you place in the snow or ice to which you can tie your rope.

Overnight Gear

If you are planning an overnight trip you will need much more gear and a larger pack. Carry a stove with fuel and a cook pot. You will need fuel for cooking as well as for melting snow to make water. In general, 0.3 liter of fuel will last one person for one day for breakfast, dinner, and melting snow.

Your sleeping bag should be a four-season mountaineering bag. Down bags are a bit more expensive but they are quite light and compress well. Unfortunately, when down bags get wet from rain or snow, they become poor insulators. Synthetic bags are generally less expensive and retain insulating properties when wet. However, they are bulky and do not compress well. Choose a bag and a temperature rating that fit your budget and needs.

A sleeping pad is also important. Much heat is lost to the ground when you sleep in the wilderness and a thick pad can keep you warm despite sleeping close to the snow. Foam pads are inexpensive, durable, and fairly comfortable. Buy one as thick as you can reasonably carry. Air mattresses are available for camping, also, but they are more expensive and useless when a hole punctures the bladder.

For short spring trips or to add warmth to a midweight bag, consider using a *bivouac sack*, an over bag that is usually windproof and waterproof. Liners for the inside of a sleeping bag can also add warmth.

Your tent will provide protection from the elements as well as a significant amount of heat. Buy a quality four-season mountaineering tent for winter trips. For spring or summer trips, a three-season tent may be adequate and is much lighter.

MAINTENANCE

Now that you have bought some backcountry equipment, you must keep it in excellent working condition. Routine maintenance and prompt repair will prolong the life of your gear, prevent field breakdown, and keep it in good resale condition, should you want to upgrade in a year or two.

Snowboard

Your snowboard is perhaps one of the most expensive tools you own and one of the most costly to repair. Routine maintenance such as waxing, edge sharpening, and repairing dings is inexpensive and can prolong the life of your board. Keep your board's edges sharp so they maintain good holding power. A hot wax will increase your glide to a smooth, fast ride. Prompt ding repair will prevent further damage from moisture or delamination. Consider having the board gone over by your local shop once or twice a season for a full tune-up, including ding repair, edge sharpening, and base grind. You can learn to do some steps yourself, which will save you a few bucks and help you repair dings sooner. Make sure you do any repair work in a well-lit, well-ventilated area, such as outside or in an open garage.

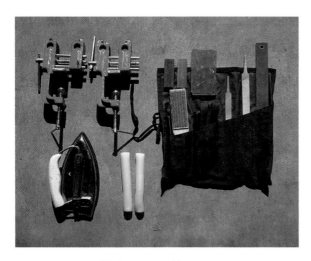

Maintenance kit

Base repair. Base repair for small dings requires using a synthetic material called *P-tex*, available at nearly any snowboard shop. First, clean the ding of wax and debris. Let the area dry thoroughly. Light a P-tex candle and allow the flame to turn blue. Eliminate as much of the black soot on the candle by letting it drip onto a metal scraper or into a metal pan. Then, allow the molten P-tex to flow into the ding. After it cools, scrape the excess so that the P-tex is level with the base. Sand or file that section of the base if needed.

TABLE 2.2: EQUIPMENT FOR SNOWBOARD MAINTENANCE AND REPAIR

Vise	Whetstone
Iron	File brush
Six-, eight-, and ten-inch files	Sandpaper
File holder	Kitchen scrub pad or wire brush
Metal scraper	P-tex
Plastic scraper	Wax

Large repairs, especially those that go through the base of the board to the core, should be handled by your local shop, as they use special tools for more durable repair. If your board has many dings consider a base grind, which will buff the entire surface.

Edge sharpening. Edges should be routinely sharpened. You will need to file both the side and base of the edge. Start with your snowboard on its side in a vise and use a six-inch file. Work from one end to the other, keeping the file flat against the edge. Run the file smoothly down the length of the board, taking care to hold the file level. After every few passes, clean the file with a wire brush. Consider using a file holder to assure that a square edge is maintained.

After both edges are filed on the side, lay your board flat upside down and file the base. An eight- or ten-inch file works best at a thirty-degree angle. Again, work from tip to tail, taking care to hold the file flat against the board to maintain a square edge. After you file the edges, you may need to remove small burrs by running a whetstone down the edge.

Wax. You may want to put a coat of wax on your snowboard to help your ride and protect the base. Choose a wax designed for the conditions of the snow or use an all-purpose wax. Speciality waxes are usually geared to either cold, dry snow or warm, wet snow. Make sure you have cleaned the base well and that it is free of dirt from filing from the edges.

Start by melting two beads of wax down the entire length of your board. Hold the waxing iron in one hand above the board and the wax stick in the other. Hold the wax against the iron so that it drips from the iron onto the board in two long beads down the center of the board. Be careful the wax does not burn and smoke. After you melt the beads of wax onto the board, use the iron flat to spread the wax evenly over the entire surface. The iron should glide smoothly over the wax on the board. Do not iron the wax off the board or touch the board's base with the iron.

After the wax dries, remove the excess with a plastic scraper so you have a smooth, even layer. Make sure you remove the wax from the edges, also. Brush in a texture or polish the wax with a nylon or wire brush or a kitchen scrubber. Small vertical lines will help your glide.

FIELD REPAIR

Geoff and I started planning about a month in advance to climb and ride the Southeast Ridge on Middle Sister in Central Oregon. We packed, peered over maps, studied guidebooks, and called the ranger.

The seven-mile approach was long and hot in mid-August and we forded three streams. At Camp Lake, 7,000 feet, we unpacked our sleeping bags and set up our small stove. After dinner, we hiked to 7,800 feet and rode down in the twilight. The sun set and the soothing alpenglow turned the snow a dusky orange and purple.

In the early morning, we climbed to the summit. We hiked on the loose volcanic rock, which ground down the plastic soles of our boots. Occasionally we hit a patch of scree: two steps up, one step back. Later, we found Irving Glacier more direct than the trail on the rocks and easier to hike. Finally reaching the 10,037-foot summit four hours later, we ate and rested. We took a few photos. Refueled and replenished, we were ready to ride.

When Geoff tried to clip in, he noticed that the front foot bail of his binding would not tighten. After some inspection we found that the plastic was worn due to seasons of hard riding and the bail would not hold. We were faced with having to hike down—not good—or having to separate while I rode and he hiked—not good, either. After a month of planning, spending money on food and maps, the long drive, short weather window, two-day hike, and mosquitoes at camp—not to mention having to work on Monday—we were not about give in easily. Staring down at 3,000 vertical feet of corn on a smooth thirty-five-degree pitch only made us want to ride all the more.

We surveyed the problem and dug out our repair kits. We rigged the bail, using a rubber strap to cinch it on top of the boot and a piece of webbing to hold it as backup against the ankle. The strap held the bail and boot tight and after a few trial turns, Geoff was sure it would hold. We carved all 3,000 feet of smooth, fast corn right up to our camp.

South Sister at twilight from high camp, Three Sisters Wilderness, Oregon

Other Gear

Your other gear mainly requires frequent checks for loose or worn parts. Try to clean everything thoroughly and allow it to dry completely after a tour. Repair or replace parts right away when you notice a problem. It may dump snow tomorrow!

Check your bindings for loose screws or worn buckles or bails. Check snowshoe bindings and baskets on your hiking poles. Boot laces can become frayed. Replace batteries in your avalanche transceiver, headlamp, and camera. Repair torn clothing promptly. Clean and reglue your climbing skins, if necessary.

Field Repair

Fixing your gear when it breaks in the field is an important skill of the backcountry. If something breaks—and it will—you should be able to fix it, at least temporarily, so you don't get stuck somewhere. You cannot carry an entire tool box, but the short list of repair materials in Table 2.1 will help you fix the most common problems. You can make many repairs with some improvisation, so think things out first.

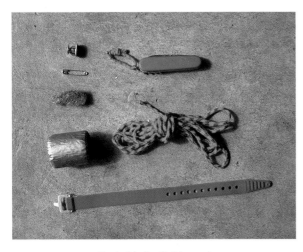

Basic kit for field repair

If you blow the threads on a binding screw, repack the hole with a small bit of steel wool. This may keep the screw tight enough for you to finish your tour. Carry an extra screw in case you lose one. A nut that fits the binding screw can be used to fix other parts on your bindings, not only where it attaches to the board.

Carry a few feet of two- or three-millimeter cord. Cord comes in handy for a shoe lace or a strap for your pole, bindings, or backpack. I also carry a rubber strap made by Voilé or a piece of webbing, which I use to repair backpack straps, snowshoe bindings, and boot laces.

A safety pin has hundreds of repair uses, especially on bindings and zippers.

Duct tape is the all-purpose repair material. Roll several feet around the shaft of your hiking pole or shovel handle so you will always have some handy. I also carry several feet wrapped around an empty plastic film canister.

A screwdriver is essential to snowboarders. Carry a pocket knife or multipurpose tool that has a #3 Phillips to tighten your binding screws.

Improvised binding repair at 9500 feet

NEW GEAR

With the growing popularity of snowboarding and backcountry riding, equipment continues to be developed. The most significant changes may be in boot and binding systems. Backcountry and mountaineering boots specifically designed for snowboarding are becoming more available. Step-in boots and bindings systems may become more interchangeable as companies license the technology to others. Fully releasable bindings may become more widely used.

Split boards, now relatively new, will likely continue to improve. Short skis may come back into popularity. Backpacks, poles, snowshoes, crampons, and other gear that is now available for backcountry snowboarders will continue to evolve to best suit our needs. Watch for new equipment each season in the magazines listed in the appendix of this book or on the Internet.

Following pages: Wolverine Cirque, Wasatch Range, Utah ©James Kay

CHAPTER THREE

MOUNTAIN SAFETY

Mountain safety should be your primary concern when in the backcountry. Many conditions can get you into trouble, such as weather, rock fall, deep snow, and avalanches. Keep in mind that mountain resorts and backcountry areas can have vastly different conditions, even on the same day in close proximity. In resort areas, professional avalanche control, grooming machines, and hundreds of skiers and snowboarders over the season create much different snowpack characteristics than those of the natural world. Also, at resorts, ski patrollers are quick to respond to injured riders and there are lodges and medical transport close by.

Because avalanche safety is so complex and essential to mountain travel, the next chapter is entirely devoted to avalanches.

GENERAL GUIDELINES

As mentioned previously, you should always follow certain basic guidelines for mountain safety and backcountry snowboarding.

Use good equipment in excellent working condition. Try to buy the best gear you can afford. Consider protective gear as well, such as a helmet for climbing and riding on treacherous terrain.

Venture into the backcountry only when you are an advanced snowboarder. You should feel comfortable with all types of terrain and snow conditions found in the backcountry. You need to be skilled at snowshoeing, free-heel skiing, or alpine climbing, depending on your preferred mode of ascent. Stay within your skill level. Hike and ride with a partner; it is more fun and safer.

Stay in good shape, both physically and mentally. Your workout regimen should be comprehensive and include stretching, aerobic workouts, and strength training such as weight lifting. If you go a long time without riding in the middle of the season, keep in shape, anyway. Make your workouts fun: bike, run, paddle, skate, or rock climb.

Spend a day or two at the resort in early season to warm up, especially if you have new gear. A new board, boots, or bindings often need to be adjusted several times when you first ride them. Ride a day at resorts in the early season to help get yourself focused and to work out the bugs after not riding all summer. Consider a *shakedown* tour—a practice session—in an area you know well, to test and adjust your new gear.

Always use good judgment. Human error contributes to many mountaineering and backcountry accidents. A forgotten piece of gear or an oversight in planning can prove to be a vital mistake. Some hazards happen in the mountain environment simply because you are in the wrong place at the wrong time. Traveling in the wilderness is never risk-free.

Seek more information. The appendix of this book contains a list of sources for more information regarding snowboarding, mountaineering, backcountry winter travel, first aid, mountain medicine, and avalanche safety. Take a course in mountaineering, backcountry travel, avalanche safety, and first aid. Consider hiring a backcountry guide for your first few tours.

ROUTEFINDING

Routefinding is one of those primary mountain skills you should learn well and practice often. Sometimes finding the route is easy, especially on a clear day in familiar terrain. But routefinding can also be extremely difficult if you get caught in a sudden storm or if the winter trail is not marked.

Route Planning

The first step in routefinding is staying found. In other words, know where you are going. This begins with good planning. Remember: snowboards are limited. You cannot go uphill or across flats without hiking, and traversing is difficult. Choose a route conducive to snow-boarding, such as a straightforward ridge climb with long, open slopes for descent that are relatively free of flat areas.

Before you head out, make sure you have a route well researched. Consult winter guidebooks and maps of the area. Talk to rangers who are familiar with the weather and terrain. Talk to locals who work in backcountry or snowboard shops and have made the tour on snowboards. Check the weather, avalanche, and road advisories. The more information you obtain ahead of time, the more fun and safe your tour will be. Call ahead several days or even weeks to start your planning.

If you are using a guidebook or winter touring map designed primarily for skiing, you may have to alter your route for a snowboard tour. This also applies if you obtain information from a ranger or local who has skied, but not snowboarded, the route. Be attentive to any mention of flat areas or routes that have many alternating up-and-down sections. You don't want to be putting on and taking off your board every five minutes.

Maps

Good maps are vital for routefinding and trip planning. The United States Geologic Survey (USGS) makes several different types. The maps that show the most detail are the USGS 7.5-minute series. These are the maps you will want to use if you get lost and need to navigate by map and compass. Other countries have comparable routefinding maps. Larger-scale maps cover a bigger area, such as an entire national park, national forest, or wilderness area. These give a complete overview of the land and roads. Some companies make winter ski and snowboard maps for popular backcountry areas, and guidebooks often have rudimentary maps. It is a good idea to get several maps covering any area in which you plan to spend time. Store the maps in resealable plastic freezer bags so they'll stay dry when out on a tour.

When looking at a map, there are several things you should note. First, check the scale. USGS 7.5-minute maps have a scale of 1:24,000, which means one inch equals 2,000 feet, less than a half mile. This information will help you gauge your hiking time. If you know that you snowshoe two miles per hour on firm snow, you can easily plan your route. Check to see when the map was most recently updated and whether it has the local magnetic declination (see "Compass Navigation," below).

Some maps have lines that correspond to direction. These lines are either noted in the margins or drawn directly on the map. North-south lines are called *longitude,* or meridians, and east-west lines are called *latitude.* Lines of latitude and longitude are numbered in minutes, seconds, and degrees, so you can identify a point on earth on any map with the longitude and latitude reading.

Routefinding maps such as the USGS 7.5-minute series also have *topographic lines,* or contour lines, that connect points of like elevation. With some practice, you will be able to look at a route on a topographic map and determine steep sections, flat areas, and major landmarks. For example, steep sections are marked by lines that are very close together. Flat sections are marked by lines that are far apart. Lines close together in a circle and ascending in elevation signify a high point, such as a peak; lines descending in elevation signify a depression, such as a dry lake.

During your hike, consult your map often. Make sure you stay on route except when making alterations as needed for safety. You should make notes on your map; for example, where a tree marks the point at which you left a ridge, or where you deviate from the standard route. Take frequent compass bearings or altimeter readings, as discussed below, in order to be able to follow your progression on the map. Keep your map handy. Pull it out every ten minutes or so to check your progress.

Compass Navigation

A map and compass are essential tools for backcountry routefinding. If you cannot see because of a whiteout, you can follow a route using a compass and readings taken from your known location on the map. This is why it is so important to always know where you are. Similarly, if you become lost or need to check your position, you can determine where you are on the map by taking readings on identifiable land formations and then plotting your location on the map. These two processes are nearly opposed to one another, and therefore will be discussed singly.

First, compasses have three main parts: an arrow, a needle, and a dial. The arrow is the pointer you use to take a bearing. The arrow is parallel to the edge of the compass and does not move. The needle always points to magnetic north. The movable dial is a protractor with directions marked out in degrees.

When using a compass you need to make adjustments between *magnetic north,* the direction in which the compass points, and *true north,* the direction upon which all maps are based. This difference between magnetic and true north is called *declination* and varies depending on where you are in the world.

Most routefinding topographic maps, such as the USGS 7.5-minute series, have the declination in degrees noted on the map. Many compasses have an adjustable declination marker that you preset for your particular area. This makes declination adjustments much easier. Some people scribe a mark on their compass for their local area. Do not forget to change the declination if you travel elsewhere.

From map to land. If you cannot see where to go, as in a whiteout or sudden storm, you can plot your travel direction on the map and use the compass as a guide. This emergency procedure can save you from getting lost or hiking off a cliff in a storm. However, you must know your position on the map, which is why keeping track of where you are at all times before the storm is so crucial. The procedure includes these

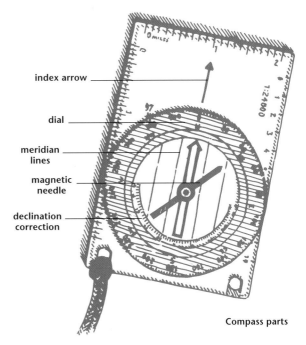

Compass parts

steps: take a map bearing, adjust for declination, and then follow the direction of travel while holding the compass in your hand. This may seem simple but actually requires lots of practice. If you are off by only a few degrees you can totally miss a road or ridge that you are aiming for. In fact, this procedure is so challenging that orienteering is a sport!

First, take a *map bearing*, a bearing from the map based on true north, by placing the compass on the map with the edge touching both your known location and

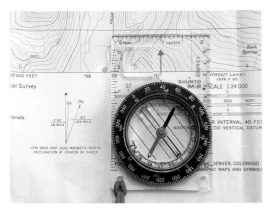

Compass with the declination scale on a USGS 7.5 minute map

the place you want to hike to. The arrow should point in your desired direction of travel on the map. Now turn the dial until the north on the dial matches north on the map. At this point, the dial should point to north on the map and the arrow should point in your travel direction. Your map bearing is read in degrees on the dial at the arrow.

Second, adjust for declination as you cannot follow the map reading until converting it to a *field bearing*, a bearing based on magnetic north. Take the compass off the map and adjust for declination by adding or

Take a map bearing by putting the edge of the compass on your known location and the place you want to hike to.

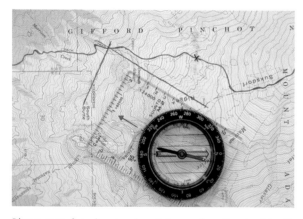

Plot a map bearing to pinpoint your location by identifying two points in the field and marking two lines on the map.

subtracting degrees. If the declination in your area is west, add degrees by turning the dial west, or counterclockwise. If the declination is east, subtract degrees by turning the dial east, or clockwise. If you have a compass with a preset declination correction, read the degrees at the designated declination mark or arrow without turning the dial.

Third, now that you have a field bearing, hold the compass horizontally in your hand, turn the entire compass, not the dial, in order that the needle is lined up with north on the dial. Now the needle and the dial point to magnetic north and the arrow points to your direction of travel. Follow this direction while holding the compass in your hand.

From land to map. When you are able to identify surrounding peaks and other landmarks, you can plot your location on the map by reversing the above steps. You need to be proficient at reading topographic maps so that you can identify landmarks both in the field and on the map. This can be a useful procedure for determining your exact location.

First, identify a landmark in the field as well as on the map. Use the map features, such as contour lines, the distance scale, and streams and roads, to help. Take a true bearing on the landmark by holding the compass horizontally in your hand and pointing the arrow at the landmark. Turn the dial so that north matches the needle pointing to magnetic north while keeping the arrow aimed at the landmark. When needle and dial point to magnetic north and the arrow points to the landmark, read the degrees at the arrow to get the field bearing.

Second, as before, you need to adjust for declination to convert a true bearing to a map bearing. To adjust a west declination, subtract the degrees by turning your dial to the east, or clockwise. To adjust an east declination, add the degrees by turning your dial to the west, or counterclockwise. Again, if your compass has a declination correction, read the degrees at the designated mark or arrow without turning the dial.

Now you have a field bearing translated to a map bearing. Place the compass with the new bearing on the map. Put the edge of the compass on the landmark you have identified on the map. Move the entire compass, not the dial, so that north on the dial points to north on the map. Draw a line on the compass edge adjacent to the landmark. You lie somewhere on this line. Repeat the steps using a different landmark. The point where the two lines intersect is your location.

Altimeter

An *altimeter* is essential in snowboard mountaineering and comes in quite handy on backcountry tours. An altimeter is a barometer that measures atmospheric pressure and then converts it to an altitude reading. As you gain altitude, you lose atmospheric pressure and vice versa. An altimeter can help you locate your elevation on a topographic map. You can mark your base camp or gauge how far you are from the summit.

The altimeter is not only affected by barometric pressure differences with altitude. Weather can change the barometric pressure and thus cause the altimeter to read incorrectly. For this reason altimeters should be calibrated daily and at places of known elevation, such as base camp or parking lots. For example, set your elevation at the parking lot on the morning you head out on your tour. Recalibrate your altimeter that evening at base camp and in the morning as well.

Because barometric pressure changes with weather, an altimeter can also help you forecast upcoming storms or fronts. A falling barometer, or rising altimeter, with no change in elevation, suggests an approaching storm. A steady or climbing barometer, with no elevation change, can mean stable weather.

Trail Markers

You may want to mark your route with wands in case of a storm or whiteout in order to find your way back down. In some cases, you may be able to make cairns. Make sure you collect all your wands on the way down and remove your cairns.

Global Positioning System

Global positioning system (GPS), is a relatively new electronic routefinding tool that pinpoints your latitude and longitude by using navigational satellites. GPS units are expensive and take some time to learn how to use efficiently. They sometimes cannot locate a satellite, such as when you are in a deep canyon. Therefore you should still carry and know how to use a map and compass.

Lost

If you do become lost, keep your head and do not panic. If it is early in the day, you should attempt to find your location and plan a route using your map and compass skills. If it is nearing dark and you cannot reasonably risk travel at night, begin preparing a *bivouac*, an unexpected emergency camp, as discussed at the end of this chapter. Hopefully you have brought along extra food, water, and clothing.

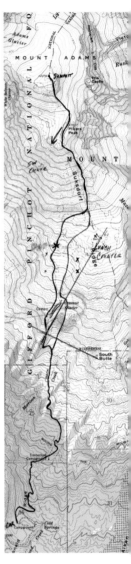

Topo map of Mount Adams, Washington marked with route

In the morning, reevaluate your situation and decide whether to attempt to hike out or wait for help. If you have left your plans with someone at home, help may be on the way. But do not count on this. Rescue is neither immediate nor automatic. Rescues can be delayed several days due to weather or avalanche hazard. You should always be prepared to spend at least one night in the wilds.

WEATHER

Weather, including sun, wind, rain, snow, ice, and cold, poses all types of hazards. Snow or rain can make travel dangerous and the trip miserable, especially if you get wet. Wind can significantly drop the temperature.

Cold

Cold is omnipresent when snowboarding and can cause injuries such as frost nip, frostbite, and hypothermia. *Frost nip* is a minor irritation to the skin due to cold, and can proceed to *frostbite* if the skin actually freezes. Signs of frostbite include numbness, pain, redness, and swelling. Often your snowboarding partner notices dull, pale, or frosted skin before you become aware of it yourself.

Hypothermia, unlike superficial injury of frostbite, occurs when the body's core temperature cools, for example, when you do not dress warmly enough; become wet from snow, rain, or sweat; or fail to eat and drink enough. Hypothermia usually presents early with shivering, cool skin, and the sensation of feeling cold. It advances to stiff muscles, slow breathing, fatigue, and incoordination. Eventually shivering stops and a feeling of warmth replaces the sensation of cold. As with frostbite, partners often notice signs of hypothermia first.

Protect yourself against cold injury in the winter and mountain environments. The requirements are fairly straightforward but often we are so focused on riding that we forget to stop and eat or drink, or fail to put on a hat or mittens when we begin to get chilled. Table 3.1 highlights general guidelines for preventing cold injury, both frostbite and hypothermia. Treatment for cold injury is discussed in Chapter Five.

Sun

The sun can be harmful as well. It can cause sunburn quite easily. *Snow blindness*, a sun injury to your eyes, often presents with severe blurred vision or even temporary blindness. Sun hazards are easy to miss when traveling on snow and in the generally cooler mountain environment. This is important to keep in mind, as sunburn and snow blindness have a delayed onset. Often red and painful sunburn occurs when you get home that evening. And if you do get snow blindness while on the mountain, it is too late to reverse the process immediately and you could be in a dangerous situation.

Prevention is straightforward and should never be discounted. Eyewear and sunscreen are two of the essentials mentioned in Chapter Two; never go without

TABLE 3.1: PREVENTION OF COLD INJURY

Wear dry, warm clothes.
Use mittens.
Put on a hat.
Wear warm, dry socks and do not lace boots too tightly.
Cover all exposed skin, especially the face with a balaclava or neck gaiter.
Regulate your body temperature using ventilation and insulating layers.
Put on extra clothes, especially a hat, when you stop for a break.
Move to generate heat. Wiggle fingers and toes, swing arms, walk.
Sit on an insulated pad or your pack.
Eat high-energy foods.
Drink warm fluids and stay well hydrated. Avoid caffeine and alcohol.
Use electric boot heaters.
Use chemical hot packs or hot water bottles. Do not put them directly on skin.
Keep out of wind and snow; get inside a tent or snow shelter.
Build a fire.
Get into sleeping bag; use two if necessary.
Watch your buddies closely for signs of cold injury.

them, no matter what the forecast is. You can get sunburnt on cloudy, overcast days, and glare can be more harmful when reflected off bright, white snow.

Protect your eyes by wearing mountaineering sunglasses with side shields or goggles. Keep your arms and legs covered during those warm summer hikes. A long-sleeved shirt, long pants, and a wide-brimmed hat will keep the direct sun off your skin. Wear waterproof sunscreen the strength of at least 15 SPF (Sun Protection Factor). Apply the sunscreen liberally and often, as it will wear off with sweat.

Storms

Storms sometimes surprise even the best weather predictors. If you get caught in a storm, protect yourself against the cold and snow. In a *whiteout*, there is almost no visibility due to thick clouds or fog, and you may need to halt progress in the middle of the day and seek shelter in a tent or snow cave. Once the storm clears or partly passes, you may be able to proceed. However, if you are in a dangerous spot such as an avalanche path, you may need to keep going until you can safely stop. This is where good judgment and planning are crucial.

Cloud cap, a collection of clouds atop a peak, can occur suddenly despite clear skies on the lower mountain. *Wind chill*, the ambient temperature adjusted for the additional cooling factor of wind on bare skin, can be colder than the actual temperature.

CLOUD CAP

It was a typical, warm summer evening: cold, clear alpine air, and dusk turning dark with tinges of pink, purple, and orange soothing the western horizon. Jennifer and I set out from Cold Springs to hike and ride Mount Adams in Washington State. The wide dirt road quickly turned into a single track, and small basalt rocks littered the trail. Every few hundred yards a cool draft drifted above patches of snow and cooled our sweaty legs. Above timberline, the trees grew smaller, more wiry; their windswept needles pointed southeast. We strapped on headlamps but left their beams off, preferring the light of the rising moon and fiery sky. Gaining elevation, we added layers of clothes. A bit later we came to the first snowfield and put on pants and gaiters. The hardening snow crunched underfoot.

By dark, we traversed Crescent Glacier and reached the first bivouacs at 8,000 feet. At Lunch Counter, 9,000 feet, we found a flat spot and unrolled our bags in the chilling night air, choosing to trade the weight of a tent for a view of night sky.

We set off at dawn after drinking a small pot of coffee and climbed Suksdorf Ridge. As we climbed, dawn became sunrise and warmed our backs. Step by heavy step, we finally reached the false summit at 11,657 feet. Clouds were blowing in from the west and within fifteen minutes had settled on the peak, blocking our view of the summit. The weather was descending rapidly and lightning sparked once.

We were only thirty minutes and six hundred vertical feet from the 12,276-foot summit. But after a short discussion we unstrapped our boards and rode down from the false summit without having bagged the peak. The ride from the false summit was still firm and fast. We hooted all the way to our overnight gear stashed at our bivouac, where the sun was still bright and warm. We looked back at the cloud cap and lightning on the summit.

The following year Jennifer and I climbed up and rode down from the top of Mount Adams on a clear, warm, sunny day. While on the summit we spied Rainier, St. Helens, and Hood standing against a crystal clear sky. We've climbed Mount Adams every year since, sometimes summiting, sometimes not.

Cloud cap on Mount Adams, Washington

Lightning

Lightning can occur nearly anytime of year, often during storms. If you get caught in a lightning storm, get to low ground and wait for the storm to end. Avoid being the highest object for lightning to strike. Be careful about taking shelter in small caves and other sheltered areas; lightning can still reach you. Try to find a large cave or overhang, or a thick grove of trees. Use your sleeping pad or pack to insulate yourself from the ground, and keep your feet close together. Stay away from metal objects. Try to wait out the storm until the lightning subsides.

HIDDEN OBSTACLES

Hidden streams, logs, and rocks are potentially dangerous, especially in early or late season when the snow cover may be light. If you fall into a cold stream on a winter day, you can become frostbitten and hypothermic quite fast. Hidden rocks and logs may lie just below the snow in early season. If you fall on one, you might bruise your tailbone or fracture your wrist. Always be cautious and alert for mountain hazards. Avoid activity in potentially hazardous terrain, such as riding on scant snow cover early in the season, or hiking up a streambed.

DEEP SNOW AND TREE WELLS

Deep snow immersion can happen to all sorts of mountain travelers. It can, however, be more dangerous for snowboarders! When riding, if you fall in deep snow—whether around a tree well, in a snowbank, or in a large, open bowl—you can land upside down. Much like the process of suffocation in an avalanche, deep snow lets in little or no air to circulate. If you are upside down in a deep, light snow, you may be unable to right yourself, and may suffocate to death.

Avoid deep snow immersion by always snowboarding with a partner and maintaining visual contact with each other at all times. Ride slopes one at a time and appoint a designated spotter for each rider. Shout for help if you anticipate a problem. If you are riding among trees or big snowdrifts, be cautious. Try to steer clear of tight trees and give tree wells a wide berth, also. Avoid snow conditions and terrain that are too difficult for your skill level, and make sure your board is long enough for deep snow. Consider riding with a pole as discussed in Chapter Seven.

Mountain hazards: deep snow and tree well in Twin Peaks Wilderness, Utah

ROCK- AND ICEFALL

Rock- and icefall are prevalent at all times of the year. Debris can fall from above when knocked by your partner or another party. Rocks and ice are sometimes dislodged by sun or wind exposure. Large amounts of snow can fall from tree limbs.

The best prevention is to avoid terrain that has rock- or icefall potential. Travel during times when rock- and icefall are minimized, such as early morning and evening hours when the snow and ice are frozen. Adjust your route to avoid hazardous areas. Avoid stopping under snow-covered trees. Wear a helmet if you must travel in areas where you are at risk of being hit by falling rocks and/or ice. Be careful when climbing not to dislodge loose rocks and ice. If something falls, yell "Rock!" to alert your partners.

HIGH ELEVATION

Acute mountain sickness (AMS), or altitude illness, is a collection of symptoms caused by low oxygen levels at high elevations. AMS is most common above 8,000 feet, which includes many backcountry areas and most ski resorts.

The main reason people get AMS is because they ascend too quickly. Many people can tolerate lower oxygen levels if they allow time to acclimate. Other factors that increase risk include dehydration, poor nutrition, getting cold, and poor physical condition.

To prevent AMS, stay well hydrated, eat regularly, keep a good pace, and rest frequently. Keep warm and dry. Stay in good physical condition. Because everyone adapts to high elevations at their own rate, good communication is extremely important.

The following are accepted general guidelines for the prevention of AMS. A key factor in prevention is to ascend slowly. Well-conditioned athletes often get severe AMS because they climb too high, too fast. Another important factor is the elevation at which you sleep. Start your tour at or below 10,000 feet if possible. Spend the first night at 10,000 feet, even if you climb higher that day. Once above 10,000 feet, your sleeping altitude should be no more than 1,000 feet per day. You can still climb more than 1,000 feet as long as you return to a lower camp. In fact, climbing a bit higher and then returning to a lower camp to sleep may help you acclimate faster. Spend a day at rest with no gain in sleeping altitude every fourth day or after every gain of 3,000 feet.

Watch closely for early symptoms of AMS, which include difficulty sleeping; headache; swollen hands, feet, and face; decreased urinary output; general weakness and fatigue; nausea; dizziness; poor appetite; and cough. More advanced symptoms include persistent headache, vomiting, difficulty breathing, shortness of breath, poor coordination, difficulty walking, and impaired concentration and judgment. In severe cases, AMS can progress to life-threatening conditions, including *high altitude pulmonary edema*, in which fluid enters the lungs, and *high altitude cerebral edema*, in which fluid enters the brain. Treatment of AMS is covered in Chapter Five.

GLACIER AND TECHNICAL CLIMBING

Glacier Travel

Glaciers, huge ice flows covering mountains in year-round snow, pose particular hazards, especially in the form of *crevasses*, or deep caverns, in the snow. One fall into a crevasse can mean a lengthy extrication by you or your partner. Snow bridges spanning crevasses easily collapse. Rockfall and avalanches are common. Also, the steep snow and ice slopes of glaciers can be hazardous for falls.

Technical climbing involves moving across any terrain that is not easily negotiated by hiking. This might mean scrambling over rocks, climbing with crampons up ice slopes, or rock climbing. Technical climbing and glacier travel are specialized areas of mountaineering beyond the scope of this book.

For safety, glacier travel usually necessitates special gear to prevent falls and slides into crevasses. As mentioned in Chapter Two, crampons for climbing will give you purchase on firm snow or ice. An ice ax will help prevent or arrest falls, should you start sliding.

If a slope is dangerous enough to require a rope for protection on the ascent,

Negotiating a crevasse on Middle Sister, Oregon

hike down—do not ride. Snowboarding in tandem with a rope is not safe and nearly impossible. Not only would it be very difficult to stop your partner from falling into a crevasse, but you would likely be dragged in as well.

Rating System

Any climbing on rock, ice, or snow is ranked with respect to technical difficulty by a number of rating systems around the world. It is worth noting these rating systems because you may come across them in guidebooks.

In North America, two main rating systems are used for technical climbing. For general climbing in North America, the *Yosemite Decimal System* is used. This system is divided into five classes. Class One is hiking. Class Two is scrambling. Class Three involves some climbing and scrambling. Class Four includes some risk of serious falls; beginners may want to have a rope with them. Class Five is any technical climbing involving a rope. Class Five is divided into subsections, from 5.0 to 5.14, ranging from easy climbing to highly technical rock climbing. Above 5.5, rock climbing skills are usually necessary.

In addition to general climbing, alpine climbing uses the *National Climbing Classification System,* which you may see more frequently in guidebooks. The overall difficulty of a route is graded from I to VI, and includes time, technical difficulty, and risks. The idea of grading is to give climbers an overview of the difficulty and time required for each climb. A Grade I climb requires a few hours; Grade II, a half day; Grade III, a full day; Grade IV, one long day with at least one section a 5.7 technical climb; Grade V, more than one day with at least one section a 5.8 technical climb; and Grade VI, over two days with advanced technical climbing.

Crescent glacier bergschrund, Mount Adams, Washington

SNOW SHELTERS

If you do need to spend an expected or unexpected night out, you should be able to build a shelter with the material at hand: snow. Some people carry tents or tube shelters for emergency. But a decent snow shelter will enable you to wait out a storm comfortably and can be warmer than a stranded vehicle or tent. Snow shelters take a few hours to build and need to be built correctly to withstand a night or two. People have been trapped in collapsed snow structures.

Snow Trench

A *snow trench* is a simple, one-person structure that is quick and easy to build. Dig a trench big enough for you to lie or sit in. It only needs to be a bit longer than you are tall and deep enough so that when you cover it, you can rest comfortably. If you are in a hurry, cover your trench with your board, poles, and snowshoes. You can stack downed branches on top for more protection. An alternative is to cut blocks from the snow with your shovel and stand them in A-frame fashion to make a tiny room. Insulate yourself from the ground with a tube shelter, plastic bag, or sleeping pad.

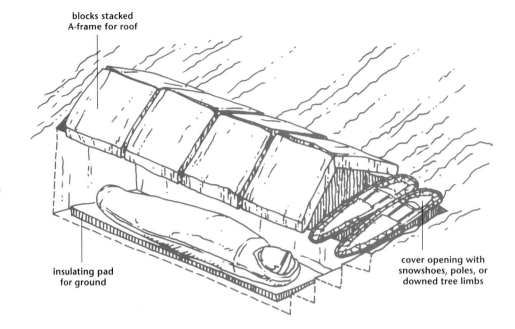

blocks stacked
A-frame for roof

Snow trench

insulating pad
for ground

cover opening with
snowshoes, poles, or
downed tree limbs

Snow Cave

A *snow cave* can be built into the side of a snow-covered hill or into a deep snowpack. For larger parties and a longer expected wait, a snow cave is more comfortable but takes longer to build than a trench. Dig a hole into the snowpack from the side or top after probing to make sure there are no hidden boulders. Dig out a hollow wide enough for two or three people. Making the door lower than the floor helps to keep cold air out. After you get in you can block the door with a pack and keep a shovel inside in case you need to dig out an entrance. Make a vent in the roof with a pole in order to get fresh air. The walls will ice up and seal you in tightly, so clear the vent periodically.

Snow cave bivouac, deep in the Twin Peaks Wilderness, Utah

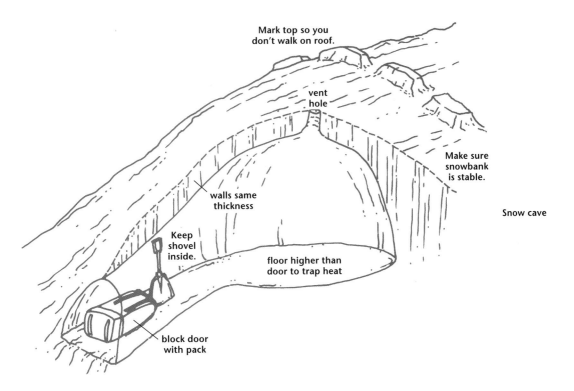

You can learn to build several other types of snow shelters, such as igloos or quinzees. For now, learn the basic types so you will be able to at least spend a night protected from an unexpected storm.

OTHER HAZARDS

This concludes the summary of the most common mountain hazards you will likely encounter. Specific geographic or geologic features in your local areas may warrant extra precautions. Be prepared for anything.

Following pages: Tasman Glacier, New Zealand ©James Kay

CHAPTER FOUR

AVALANCHE SAFETY

The first avalanche death of a snowboarder occurred in 1986 near Brighton, Utah. Since avalanches are ubiquitous in the mountains, they pose one of the most significant hazards. Avalanches have injured and killed athletes of all ability levels, from novices to experts. Along with the rise of snowboarding, the number of deaths of snowboarders due to avalanches is increasing, as shown in Table 4.1.

The primary goal of avalanche safety is avoidance. In this chapter, avalanche terrain, avalanche weather, and characteristics of the snowpack are discussed in detail. All three features play an integral part in safe travel in avalanche country.

Information presented in this chapter is meant to be only a beginning to your understanding of avalanches. Supplement these pages with one of the books on avalanches listed in the appendix, as well as a Level One avalanche course.

BEFORE YOU GO

A complete pretour checklist is highlighted in Chapter Six. However, in regard to avalanches, it is worth mentioning a few things you should get into the habit of doing every time you head out.

Check the weather report and avalanche advisory. Most mountain areas have a local avalanche report that can give you general information and a general risk assessment. However, the avalanche report and weather forecast are only basic information, and often cover a large geographic area.

Assimilate the avalanche and weather information into your knowledge of the entire season's snowpack and weather conditions. It would be foolhardy to travel to an area, check one day's advisory, and head out. If new to an area, check with locals in backcountry shops, as well as rangers.

On the drive up to the mountains look for signs of new snow and recent avalanches. If you run into other snowboarders or skiers in the parking area, find out where they are going and what they know about the weather and snow conditions.

Check everyone's beacon to make sure they are all functioning and on the 457kHz frequency. The easiest way to do this is have one person switch to "receive" and walk across the parking lot, just out of range. Then, one by one, each member of your group walks toward that person with their beacons on "transmit." The receiving person should be able to pick up everyone's signal from a good distance. The receiving person should then switch places with the last person to check that beacon as well. If you have time, a quick beacon search drill will keep everyone's skills sharp.

Plan your route acording to the safety level of the conditions, the skill level of everyone in your party, and the mode of ascent.

Lastly, if no terrain is safe, stay home or abandon the tour. Aborting a tour even minutes from a summit may be one of the smartest moves you ever make. Many times, I have packed and been ready to go, only to awaken in the morning to find conditions poor. Turning around is disappointing, but your life is worth more than a day of fresh tracks.

Cornice, Brighton back bowls, Utah

AVALANCHE TERRAIN

Avalanche Types

Avalanches are usually one of four types: slab, point-release, cornice, and ice. A *slab avalanche* is a strong, cohesive layer of the snowpack that fractures and slides all at once over a weaker layer underneath. These are usually the big slides that occur during or after a storm in the winter. Most fatal avalanches are slabs that are triggered by the people they kill.

A *point-release avalanche* is an area of loose snow that releases from a single point. As it slides, this type of avalanche gathers snow and grows larger. Point-release avalanches most often occur in the spring, when the warm afternoon sun softens the snow.

A *cornice* is a thick snow outcrop on a ridge generated by persistent wind. When a cornice breaks, it falls in a heap and can slide some distance or even trigger a slab avalanche. Similarly, an *ice avalanche* occurs when consolidated ice becomes unstable and collapses.

Slab avalanche, Tanners Slide, Little Cottonwood Canyon, Utah

Avalanches have a starting zone, a track, and a run out. The *starting zone* is where the avalanche begins to slide. The *track* is the area the avalanche slides along before stopping. The *run out* is the point at which the avalanche stops. Run outs are often a long way from the starting zone—in the big mountains, frequently miles away. This means that even if you are traveling on a shallow-angled slope, safe from triggering a local slide, you could get hit from a slope far above you.

Slope Angle

Avalanches most often slide on slopes of twenty-five to fifty degrees. The greatest danger for human-triggered slides comes from a slope between thirty-five and forty degrees, with thirty-eight degrees the most common angle for slab avalanches. Steeper slopes do not hold snow, and shallower-angled slopes do not build up the momentum to slide. Also, convex slopes are usually more hazardous than concave slopes.

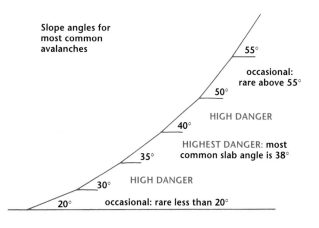

Slope angles for most common avalanches

55°
occasional: rare above 55°
50°
HIGH DANGER
40°
HIGHEST DANGER: most common slab angle is 38°
35°
HIGH DANGER
30°
20°   occasional: rare less than 20°

Anchors

Open bowls are the most likely spots for avalanches to occur. Anchors such as trees and rocks, if partially buried and spaced tightly, can help prevent a slope from sliding. In general, if the trees are too thick to ride through and hiking is difficult, these anchors provide some stability.

Large rocks and groups of trees on an otherwise open slope can provide *islands of safety*. If the slope slides, the area around the trees or rocks may not, and at least may provide you with something to grab hold of if you get caught.

Aspect

Aspect, or orientation, of the slope influences slope stability. In the Northern Hemisphere, south-facing slopes get the most direct sun exposure. Direct sun and heating can significantly alter the snowpack characteristics (see "Avalanche Weather" below). In the spring, warm temperatures and direct sun cause dramatic warming, and point-release slides occur.

The shaded north-facing slopes are usually cooler and snowpack is often deeper. In winter, avalanche danger may persist for a long time without the help of the sun's rays to consolidate the snowpack. This is why many days after a storm the best snow is often on the shaded north-facing slopes.

Local Geography

Like aspect, local geography impacts avalanche hazard. The Rocky Mountains, for example, have different weather, snow, and terrain characteristics compared to the Sierra Nevada or Cascade Ranges. You should be familiar with local wind patterns and storm tracks. Also, try to find a local source, such as a ranger station or avalanche forecast center, that can identify common avalanche paths.

Terrain Traps

Avalanches do not have to be large to kill you. *Terrain traps*, small areas like narrow gullies and streambeds, are prone to small avalanches. Even these small slides can bury you. Small avalanches can also carry you into trees and rocks, over cliffs, and into crevasses. Think not only about if the slope will slide, but about what will happen to you if it does.

AVALANCHE WEATHER

Not only does weather bring snow, but wind, sun, temperature, rain, and other meteorologic changes dramatically affect the snow. Keep in mind that weather is a continuum. Follow the weather all winter. Learn typical patterns in your area as this will help you predict weather.

Snow

New snow in the mountains is a primary cause of avalanches. In fact, most natural slab avalanches happen during or immediately following storms. The new snow takes time to bond to the existing snowpack. In general, the more snow and the faster it falls, the greater the danger and the longer the area will take to stabilize. Be on guard, especially if it begins snowing during your tour, or if it snows an inch an hour or more.

Wind

Wind is only second to storms in terms of its impact on snow stability. The wind moves a large amount of snow in a short time. In fact, wind sometimes brings more snow to a slope than a storm.

In North America, the prevailing west wind moves snow from west to east. Hence east-facing slopes are often snow-loaded by wind and more dangerous during or following windy days. West-facing slopes are often wind-scoured and sometimes safer.

If you are accustomed to one wind direction always loading certain slopes, a change in direction caused by a local weather disturbance requires extra caution and evaluation. During the day the wind may pick up or change directions. Ridge tops may be windy when lower canyons or valleys are not.

Temperature and Sun

Long periods of cold temperatures inhibit stabilization of the snowpack. Cold temperatures following a storm often cause the danger of avalanche to persist and hamper the snowpack's tendency to consolidate and strengthen.

Sun and heat can both increase and decrease stability of the snowpack. Immediately after a storm, rapid heating from the sun may cause instability. However, in the week following a storm, gradual heating can promote bonding of snow crystals and help the snowpack to consolidate and stabilize more quickly.

In the spring and summer, the hot sun melts the bonds and again promotes instability and point-release avalanches.

Rain

Initially, rain adds weight to the snowpack without adding much strength. Later, cold temperatures can freeze the rain-soaked snowpack into a hard, stable crust. This crust can turn into a slick surface on which a slab might slide.

THE SNOWPACK

When snow falls in the mountains, it does not merely lie there. It changes—sometimes rapidly, sometimes slowly. There are three basic types of snow changes: rounding, faceting, and the melt-freeze cycle.

In the following discussion, strength of the snow usually refers to a strong or weak layer. The snowpack is usually not homogeneous, but layered from multiple storms over the season. A strong layer does not mean a safe or stable snowpack. Many avalanches occur when a very strong, cohesive layer slides on a weak layer.

Point release avalanche, Wolverine Cirque, Utah

Rounding

Rounding is a type of snow metamorphosis that creates strongly bonded, rounded crystals, also called *equilibrium form*. The previous name for this was equitemperature metamorphosis because it is a change that occurs when the snowpack is the same temperature throughout, and most often, when temperatures are warmer. This metamorphosis, called *sintering*, takes place when the crystals stick together with strong bonds. This snow packs together well and makes good snowballs. This strong layer of snow forms slabs in the winter.

AVY 101

When I first heard about an avalanche course for snowboarders, I was hesitant. It was difficult to get a three-day weekend completely free. Plus, the class cost a few bucks and I'd have to make a commitment almost a month in advance. And then, what if there was epic powder that day and I was trudging around in the snow?

The course I took was run by Friends of the Utah Avalanche Forecast Center and was taught by snowboarders to snowboarders. Base camp was the Wasatch Mountain Club Lodge in Brighton, Utah. Each day included didactic talks before heading out into the field.

The first day, we practiced avalanche rescue, including beacon searches. Although I had practiced before, nothing had ever come close to the simulated rescues in that course. At first our group rescued the buried beacon in twelve minutes. I knew someone could die easily in only four minutes—and we had four people searching! By the end of the day and many searches later, we were routinely finding the buried beacon in less than four minutes.

The second day, we discussed snow stability. We dug pits and analyzed the snowpack. At the end of the day we hiked to the top of Mount Wolverine and rode down smoothly in loud powder. We spent the third day hiking and riding, using our routefinding and snow-stability evaluation skills. We hiked to Catherine Pass, where the turns were so fine that we hiked back up to Powder 8 Hill for another run.

Courses are given throughout the United States and the world. No matter how many books I read or how often I practice on my own, nothing has ever quite equaled that Level One course.

Faceting

Faceting, also called recrystallization, is a type of snow metamorphosis that creates weakly bonded, faceted crystals, also called *kinetic growth form.* Faceting was formerly known as temperature gradient metamorphosis because it occurs when the snowpack has a significant temperature difference, for example, when the snowpack is warmer near the ground and colder on the surface. It most often occurs with prolonged cold temperatures.

Unlike rounded grains, faceted grains do not form strong bonds and usually create a persistently weak layer in the snowpack. Because this snow does not bond and consolidate, good riding lasts for several days after a storm. This recrystallized, faceted snow is also called *sugar snow* or *loud powder*. Because of its light and unbonded consistency, this snow sparkles in the sun and makes for great, fast riding.

When this weak layer of faceted snow persists and is buried by other layers, it is called *depth hoar*. A common occurrence is a thick, strong layer of rounded grains from a new storm sliding on a thin, weak layer of faceted grains that persisted from many days of cold, clear weather preceding the storm.

Melt-Freeze Cycle

The third main type of metamorphosis is the *melt-freeze cycle*. This occurs most often in spring when temperatures drop below freezing at night, and then warm to above freezing during the day. The snow crystals are connected by water bonds. When the air temperature drops below freezing at night, the bonds freeze and the snowpack strengthens to a firm crust. When the temperature warms to above freezing during the day, the bonds melt and the snowpack weakens to *slush*, or dense, wet snow.

Somewhere between the frozen crust and the melted slush is *corn*. Corn occurs when the first few inches of snow soften but the crust still supports a snowboarder. Later in the day, the snow turns to slush, and it is during this time that point-release slides occur in the weakened snowpack. Later in the spring, the snowpack may not freeze overnight, yielding persistent slush.

Other Layers

A few other types of snow are worth noting, mostly for identification purposes as they can be dangerously weak layers when buried. Again, the main point of learning about all these snow layers and types is to know that there are weak ones and strong ones. The strong layers are cohesive and can slide on the weak, buried layers.

Surface hoar, or *hoar frost,* is a type of crystal that forms from frozen dew on the surface of the snowpack.

Rime is a layer of snow or ice that forms when supercooled water vapor in the air condenses on the surface of the snow or on trees.

Crust, a hard, firm layer, originates from rain, sun, rime, or wind exposure that usually overlies softer snow.

Graupel, a round, hail-like snow, sometimes falls in midwinter storms.

Sastrugi is wind-eroded snow in the form of ridges and waves.

Sastrugi

Ice comes in many forms, such as *verglas*, a transparent, thin ice layer on rocks, *blue ice*, or solid ice, and *gray ice*, which is extremely hard snow.

Firn, or *névé*, is hard, consolidated snow formed by repeated melt-freeze cycles, and is usually found on permanent snowfields and glaciers in the summer.

SNOWPACK EVALUATION

Oftentimes, despite numerous layers, the snowpack may be stable. This is when your knowledge comes into play. Your goals are to distinguish between and evaluate strong and weak layers, to estimate the stability of the snowpack, and to plan your tour accordingly. When hiking and riding in avalanche terrain, you should constantly reevaluate the snowpack for stability. Use all your senses and alter your route according to your findings.

Look, Listen, Feel

Feel the snowpack under your feet. Some sensations you may experience include a hollow feel or sound to the snow, cracks shooting out from your skis or snowshoes, or a loud *wumph* noise when one layer of snow collapses upon another. These signs suggest significant instability, so you should seek safer ground immediately.

Look around for signs of avalanche activity. The most obvious warning is evidence of recent avalanches, including debris or a fracture line on a hillside. Fractured trees, or *flagging*, when the uphill branches are gone from a tree, can be a sign of a slide path. An area of downed timber with stands on either side often marks an avalanche path.

Watch how the snow falls into the trail after you or your partner breaks through. If large chunks break off, the snow may be less stable. You should step just above your partner's track to observe how easily the snow falls into the trail. If one hiker is always breaking trail, everyone else should step into the untracked snow to hike for a few minutes. This will allow everyone to get a feel for the firmness of the snow.

Dig

Your best source of information for snowpack evaluation is to dig into it. The easiest way is to probe quickly at the snow with your pole or a scoop of your hand. As explained above, you are trying to get to know the snowpack. Suppose you are touring on a few inches of fresh snow over a relatively hard crust. By taking a swipe at the snow every few minutes, you might find areas of wind-loaded or wind-scoured snow, or areas where the snow is thicker and more dense.

Snow pit. The standard method for examining layers and evaluating the stability of the snowpack is to dig a *snow pit*. This takes fifteen minutes and can give you lots of information. Dig a good-sized pit, at least four feet by four feet in area. Make sure it is on a slope that is safe and has the same angle and aspect that you

Checking the layers in a snowpit *Shovel shear test* *Compression test*

want to test. For example, if you are going to ride a forty-degree, north-facing slope, dig a pit on a forty-degree, north-facing slope. Depending on the conditions and how well you know the terrain, weather, and snowpack, you might dig several pits during the day at several locations.

When evaluating the snow, first check for layers visually. Scan the pit and run a gloved hand over its walls to find the layers. You can push on layers to check for hardness using the following rough scale: fist—very soft; four fingers—soft; one finger—medium; pencil—hard; and knife—very hard. Look for weak layers, such as depth hoar, crust, or graupel, and note their depths and thicknesses. If you have been digging pits and watching the weather all season, several of the layers should look and feel familiar to you. You might even keep a notebook to record your findings. Next, you should check several tests to evaluate the layers' cohesion to each other.

Shovel shear test. The *shovel shear test* is one of the standards. Isolate a column of snow in your pit about one foot by one foot or the width of a standard avalanche shovel. Isolate the sides and back by cutting into the snow with your shovel. Then place your shovel blade at the back of the column and gently pull forward, toward you. The column will slide at the weakest point. Note how much pressure is needed to obtain the fracture and at which layer it slides.

Compression test. Since the shovel test is somewhat difficult to quantify, the *compression test* is sometimes more useful. Isolate another one-by-one-foot column. Place your shovel blade flat on top of the column. First, tap the shovel against the column by bending your hand at the wrist. If the column fractures, it is very unstable. If it does not fracture, tap it a few more times. Then tap the column a few times by swinging your forearm at the elbow. If the column still does not slide, tap it by swinging your arm at the shoulder. The more force you need to fracture the column, the more stable it is. The compression test is usually quantified by the number of taps necessary and with which joint you had to swing your arm. For example, two taps bending the wrist is very unstable. Several taps from a full swing of the arm at the shoulder is more stable.

Another type of shovel compression test uses a stuff sack filled with snow instead of your arm. Fill the sack with ten pounds of snow, using a portable scale to measure the weight. Then drop the sack from various heights and note at which height the block fails.

Tilt board test. Another pit test, the *tilt board test*, is useful to quantify stability. Cut a block of snow the same width and length as your shovel blade. Scoop up the block and then tilt the shovel blade. The steeper the angle at which you tilt the shovel blade, the more stable the snow is.

Other pit tests. Any interaction with the snow will provide helpful information. Pick up blocks after they slide off the column and break them over your knee. This will help you gauge how dense those layers are. Stack blocks on an isolated column to estimate how much new snow might be needed to make the column slide. Use your hands instead of a shovel to break the column as this may give you a better feel for the snowpack.

Rutscheblock test. The final test in your pit is the *Rutscheblock test,* which takes a little more time but can give you more information on the overall strength of the snowpack. Isolate a column of snow large enough to stand on with your snowboard. Use your shovel, the tail of your board, or a snow saw to isolate a six-by-six-foot block. Once it is cut, climb around to the top of the slope. Step onto the block wearing your skis, snowshoes, or split board in ski mode. If you are using a snowboard, place the board on the block and then step into the bindings.

If the block slides while you are cutting or stepping onto it, or while you flex your leg a few times on the top of it, the snow is unstable. After you flex your leg, jump on the block. If you are able to make only one or two jumps before the block fails, the slope is possibly unstable. If you make several jumps and the block does not move, the slope is probably relatively stable— at least, according to this test—and you should incorporate this information into other observations. Remember: once the block fails, check how deeply and on which layer the fracture occurs. The block should slide at one of the layers you noted in the shovel shear or compression tests.

Reutscheblock test

Test

Test slopes. With more skill you can try riding *test slopes*. Test slopes are short hills, usually allowing only three or four turns, with the same aspects and snow conditions as the one you want to ride. Good test spots are often road banks or collections of snow located alongside tree stumps. Ride test slopes to ascertain how stable they are. Use extra caution as no slope, even a short one, is totally safe.

Ski cuts. Experienced mountain travelers know how to make *ski cuts*, which also gauge the stability of the snow and minimize risks. A ski cut is a single traverse across the crest of a slope that entails riding from one island of safety to another.

SAFE TRAVEL

Once you evaluate the weather, snowpack, and terrain, you are on your way to preventing avalanches. Remember the three factors: weather, snowpack, terrain. You can't change weather patterns and snowpack characteristics, but you can change your route and decrease the risk of avalanches by choosing safer terrain. Sometimes this means that no terrain is safe, and that you should abandon the tour, or not even start out.

One of the cardinal rules is to avoid slopes thirty degrees or steeper if the possibility of avalanche danger is high. Measure slopes with a clinometer before you hike them. After a while, you will be able to quickly estimate the slope angle and will have developed an eye for dangerous ones.

An essential avalanche skill: checking slope angle with clinometer

Avoid hiking up open slopes. The safest areas to hike on are broad ridges. You should generally hike on the windward side of the ridge to avoid a wind-loaded cornice. A cornice can fracture several feet back from the lip. Stick to areas with thick trees.

Be careful of terrain traps like short, steep couloirs, riverbeds, and cliffs. Do not hike in streambeds, but above them.

If you need to cross a potential avalanche path, always do so one person at a time and hike from one island of safety to another. Always stay in visual and voice contact with everyone in your party. Designate a spotter for each person before he or she hikes a potentially dangerous area. Avoid stopping until you are in a safe area.

If you hike the low path across a potentially dangerous slope, hike as far from the run out as possible. If you hike the high path, hike as high as possible above the starting zone.

If you have a small day pack, tighten the straps. If you get caught in a slide, the pack will help you float and protect your back. If you have a large pack or a board strapped to your pack, consider unbuckling the waist belt so you can get rid of it if you are caught in a slide. That large or heavy an item could weigh you down. Remove pole straps from your wrists. Make sure you are not wearing a snowboard leash; if you need to get out of your board, you want to be able to do so quickly. Bundle up before you ride. Put on your gloves, goggles, and hat or hood.

When riding, the same guidelines apply as when hiking: always proceed one at a time, stay in visual contact, and designate a spotter. When only one person rides, there is less stress on the snowpack, and if the slope does slide, everyone else will be needed for rescue.

Carefully crossing a potentially dangerous slope, Flagstaff Mountain, Utah

Make the first run next to the trees on the edge of the slope. That way, you are close to an escape, if needed. When you stop, choose a safe place out of the path of a potential slide. Do not stop in the middle of the slope.

Make sure everyone in your party feels comfortable with the snow and slope conditions. Many avalanches are triggered when riders fall.

Continually evaluate conditions throughout your tour, all the way back to your car. Choose a safe campsite if you are staying overnight.

IF YOU ARE CAUGHT

When primary avalanche precautions fail, even skilled backcountry travelers get caught. Sometimes we push the limits of safe travel or miss important warning signs. Peer pressure often forces us into dangerous situations. People die in avalanches either from traumatic injuries caused by the slide or from suffocation upon being buried. Hopefully you are following precautions. If you are caught in a slide, you will be able to execute some key maneuvers.

If you are riding first, you should be the only person in your party caught in a slide, since you are riding one at a time. Everyone else should be watching you. Shout "Avalanche!" at the top of your lungs to make sure they see you. Try to stay on your feet and ride out to the side immediately. Do not try to outrun the avalanche; no matter how fast you are, it will overcome you. If you are knocked down, try to stop by digging into the surface of the snow or grabbing onto a nearby rock or tree. Keep your feet pointing downhill and your board facing front for protection from trees or rocks.

Taking a mid-morning break beneath Cardiff Pass, Utah

If you slide with the avalanche, close your mouth and breathe through your nose, if possible, to keep snow out of your mouth and throat. As stated above, keep a day pack on as it will help you float and protect your back, but try to remove a heavier backpack and snowboard. Skiers should try to get rid of skis and poles. If you are snowboarding, you probably will not have time to remove your board, even if you have step-in bindings.

Fight with all your might to stay near the surface. Try to swim to the top of the debris by swinging your arms. The idea is to struggle to stay close to the surface of the snow to avoid deep burial when the slide comes to a halt.

When the snow begins to slow, push one hand to the surface to alert searchers to your location. A visual fix is much faster than a beacon search. Use the other hand to clear as much snow as possible from in front of your face. This small air pocket will give you some time before you run out of air.

If you are partially buried, dig yourself out so others can search for anyone else who might be caught. If you are totally buried, keep calm to save energy and air.

RESCUE

When an avalanche buries someone, time is critical. Most people who get caught are saved by rapid rescue by their touring partners. Rarely does anyone survive avalanche burial longer than thirty minutes. Always search rapidly but systematically, as the buried person is quickly running out of air.

TABLE 4.1: DEATHS OF SNOWBOARDERS BY AVALANCHE IN THE UNITED STATES OVER THE PAST TEN YEARS, INCLUDING BACKCOUNTRY SNOWBOARDERS AND RESORT SNOWBOARDERS RIDING OUT OF BOUNDS

Year	Deaths
1985–86	1
1986–87	0
1987–88	0
1988–89	0
1989–90	1
1990–91	0
1991–92	0
1992–93	3
1993–94	0
1994–95	3
1995–96	4
1996–97	3
1997–98	4

Hasty Search

If your partner is caught, the first step is to watch for him or her closely. Often you can see exactly where the person is located, or at least the general area. Once the slide stops, make sure that further slides are not coming down before you head onto the debris. Safety of rescuers is paramount. If you have a large group, consider appointing one person to watch for slides from above in order to warn other rescuers.

Mark the last-seen point of the victim with a pole or snowshoe. Quickly search the area for visible or audible clues, such as a piece of clothing or a board sticking through the snow. Quickly probe likely spots below the last-seen point, such as in tree wells and above rocks. You may be able to locate a buried person immediately. If the individual is not found quickly with a hasty search, start a beacon search.

Beacon Search

The beacon search is usually broken down into three sections: signal location, grid search, and fine search. Conventional beacons grow louder the closer you are to the victim, but they do not show direction or distance.

Signal location. Turn your beacon on to "receive" at its loudest reception. Make sure everyone in your party is also on "receive" so as not to get a false signal from someone who is not buried. Remember to watch for additional avalanches, and be ready to turn your beacon back to "transmit" if a second slide comes.

Practicing the beacon search

Begin a rough search of the debris below the person's last-seen point. With one rescuer, traverse the slope from side to side until you pick up the signal. With two or more rescuers, you can walk down the slope fifty feet apart. You may need to change the position of the beacon in your hand in order to get the loudest reception. If your beacon also has a light indicator, use it in conjunction with the sound.

If for whatever reason you cannot pick up the original signal, repeat this initial step of the search several times.

Grid search. Once you pick up the signal, one person should begin the grid search while the others ready probes and shovels. As needed, turn down the volume the closer you get because your ear is more sensitive to signal changes at low volumes. Also, keep the beacon at the same angle and direction to the slope throughout your search.

Start walking down the slope. The signal should become louder, then quieter. Retrace your steps to find the loudest point. Then turn ninety degrees and begin walking across the slope. The signal will again grow loud, then quiet. You should walk in both directions, right and left, until you home in on the loud spot. From the loud spot, turn ninety degrees and make a third pass up and down the slope. Find the loud point and make a fourth pass across the slope. After four or five passes, you should be able to home in on the general burial point in the snow within a few feet.

Fine search. Get on your knees and use your beacon next to the snow for the fine search. Use a grid pattern up and down, then right and left. Mark the spots

Avalanche beacon rescue: locate signal and grid search

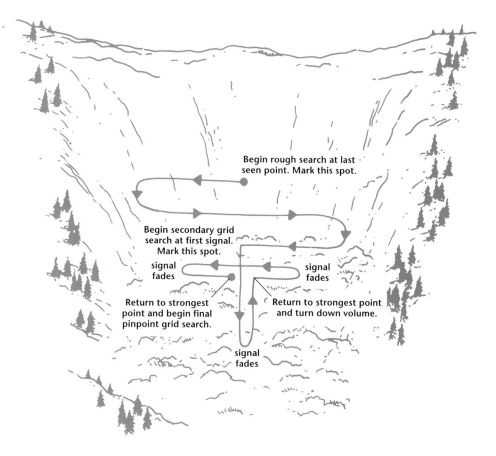

Begin rough search at last seen point. Mark this spot.

Begin secondary grid search at first signal. Mark this spot.

signal fades

signal fades

Return to strongest point and begin final pinpoint grid search.

Return to strongest point and turn down volume.

signal fades

where the beacon fades; the signal should be loudest in the middle of this area. If the person is buried near the surface, you should be able to arrive at an exact location. If the person is buried deep, you may get a square a few feet across without any specific loud spot.

Probe and dig. Before you start digging, probe the snow to pinpoint the person's exact location. Be careful not to dig too aggressively or you might injure the person you are trying to save. But dig quickly. Get the victim's head uncovered first, then dig out the rest of the body. Certain injuries, such as spinal or head trauma or if the person is not breathing, require extra precaution and attention, as explained in Chapter Five.

Induction method. The *induction* or *tangent method* is an advanced, alternative method that can be used for the secondary search instead of the grid pattern. You will still use the traditional search pattern for the signal location and the fine search.

Induction is based on magnetic lines that radiate from the buried person. After you have located the initial signal, hold the beacon parallel to the snow. Aim the beacon from ninety degrees right to ninety degrees left and home in on the strongest signal. Once you have found the strongest point, walk the direction in which the beacon is pointing for fifteen feet. Sweep the beacon again and follow it for another fifteen feet. When the signal weakens, retrace your steps to the last loud point and begin to plot a fine grid.

This advanced technique can be faster but requires a great deal of practice. If it fails, revert to the traditional grid pattern.

Probe Line

If you cannot find the buried person after several attempts with the beacon, you may need to probe. You must organize the probe in a systematic manner to avoid missing the victim. Arrange several people at arm's length from one another, each with a probe. First everyone probes to their right, then center, then left, with each probe point about a foot apart. All the rescuers should take one step forward and probe right, center, and left again. This continues in order to cover the area in which you suspect the person is buried.

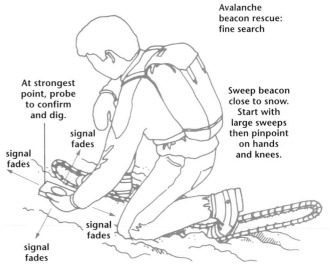

Avalanche beacon rescue: fine search

At strongest point, probe to confirm and dig.

Sweep beacon close to snow. Start with large sweeps then pinpoint on hands and knees.

signal fades

signal fades

signal fades

signal fades

Going for Help

Above all, keep in mind the safety of the rescuers. Delay in making the decision about when to go for help. The best resource is a quick rescue by the buried person's partner or partners.

NEW IDEAS

Digital beacons are now available. These have computer chips that give direction and approximate distance of the buried person. Similarly, experiments are underway for using the global positioning system in avalanche searches.

In Europe, avalanche air bags are becoming available. These are backpack-mounted air bags that inflate with a nitrogen cartridge when the user pulls a rip cord. They allow the victim to float closer to the surface of the snowpack, and help to avoid total burial, both lessening injuries and speeding rescue.

RECCO is a small diode that is sewn into clothing and/or glued to gear. To use RECCO to find an injured person, you need to have a microwave unit that sends out a signal that bounces off the strip and returns to the unit. Some ski patrols are using these, but not widely in the backcountry, as it is not practical for a local search to carry the large locating unit.

CHAPTER FIVE

FiRST AiD

First aid, like avalanche rescue, is something you hope never to need. But injury and illness do occur; they are part of the risks of the backcountry. Sometimes there is an oversight in preparation or you make a mistake. Other times you are in the wrong place at the wrong time.

Taking care of even minor injuries in the field can speed healing and prevent complications. This is why it is important for all backcountry snowboarders to have at least some general first-aid skills. This chapter is not a substitute for a first-aid course, which provides you with the knowledge and skills to take care of a wide variety of backcountry injuries and illnesses. The best course offered is Mountaineering Orientated First Aid (MOFA), which is specifically focused on mountain and winter environments. Basic life support, or cardiopulmonary resuscitation (CPR), is taught by local chapters of the American Red Cross, community colleges, mountaineering clubs, or other local organizations. A variety of first-aid books specifically geared to mountaineers are listed in the appendix.

PREVENTION

To minimize risk of injury and illness, good planning and preparation are paramount. Every time you head out to the backcountry, you take a risk. The idea is to be comfortable with an acceptable level of risk and to minimize potential problems. The safety guidelines discussed in Chapter Three are briefly reviewed below.

Use good equipment in excellent working condition. Wear protective gear such as a helmet when climbing and riding in exposed terrain. Seek instruction, practice, and experience in backcountry travel. Know basic safety and survival skills. Stay in good physical condition. Be cautious and use good judgment. Watch for cold and sun injury. Be on guard for mountain hazards such as storms, lightning, hidden obstacles, deep snow, rock- and icefall, and high elevation.

FIRST-AID KIT

A first-aid kit is part of your essential equipment. You can buy one at your local backcountry store or gather the materials yourself. The size of the kit depends on a number of variables. If you typically go out on day tours relatively close to roads, take a kit designed for a day outing. These usually are compact and include supplies for small wounds. If, typically, you spend a night or two in the backcountry and travel to places somewhat remote and removed from help, you should take a larger kit. If you are part of a big group, carry a large kit or several

A well-stocked first aid kit

small kits in order to have multiple supplies. See Table 5.1 for recommendations for a basic first-aid kit.

You should learn how to use everything in your kit, which is why taking a class and reading a book on first aid are so beneficial and important. Also, carry a compact first-aid book so you can review the skills when necessary.

TABLE 5.1: RECOMMENDED ITEMS FOR A BASIC FIRST-AID KIT

Small irrigation syringe	Compact first-aid book
Antiseptic cleanser	Sunscreen
Antibiotic ointment	Water purification tablets
Nonadherent dressing	Gloves and CPR microshield
Gauze pads, various sizes	Safety pins
Adhesive bandages, various sizes	Splint
Butterfly bandages	First-aid tape, waterproof
Liquid bandage	First-aid tape, cloth
Moleskin	Elastic wrap, two-inch width

Anti-inflammatory pain medicine, such as ibuprofen or aspirin
Oral rehydration solution, powdered form

INJURY ASSESSMENT

Organize and Take Charge

When an injury occurs, however minor, you should approach the situation in a stepwise fashion. This will keep you organized and efficient. Stay calm, as you will be best able to help yourself or someone else if you keep your head. One person should take charge quickly and organize your group for maximum efficiency. This responsibility usually falls on the person with the most backcountry and first-aid experience.

Prevent Another Accident

The second step in successful first aid is to prevent additional accidents. If someone is injured in a dangerous area, do not approach him or her until you can do so in safety. This especially holds true for avalanche rescue. Many times rescuers have been injured by subsequent avalanches. Before administering first aid, you may need to move the injured person to a safe place, as in the cases of an avalanche or a crevasse fall. The exceptions are potential head or spine injuries. In these cases, you should not move an injured person unless you have experience with head and spine immobilization, as discussed later.

Evaluate

Next, evaluate the injured person. With major injuries you should first complete a primary survey, including airway, breathing, and circulation—ABC—in that order. First check the airway. Clear it of snow and debris. Then check if the person is breathing. Note if the chest is moving up and down or if air is coming from the mouth and nose. Third, check circulation by looking for a pulse in the neck and checking the skin to see if it is warm and pink. If any of the above signs are absent, you will likely need to start CPR, if you are trained. Again, if there is risk of head or spine injury, you need to immobilize the patient to prevent further trauma.

After the primary survey, do a secondary survey of the entire body and injured areas. Make sure you check out the injured person completely, from head to toe. Look for bruising, deformity, bleeding, and evidence of pain—all signs of significant injury. Often you can focus on particular body parts and injuries, such as a sprained ankle or twisted knee. But be careful not to overlook more subtle injuries masked by the pain of larger ones.

Treat

Initiate first-aid treatment. The person with the most first-aid experience should take care of assessment and treatment. With falls, this is usually wound care or caring for a sprain or fracture of the arm or leg, as outlined later in this chapter.

Prevent Further Injury

Do not forget that you are in the wilderness. Not only should you care for the initial injury, you should prevent sun and cold injury as well. Injured people are more susceptible to hypothermia, frostbite, and acute mountain sickness. Dress the injured person in warm clothes, especially a hat. Insulate the person from the cold snow by using a pack as a seat. Consider preparing a hot drink.

Evacuate

Finally, make a plan. The plan should be decided by the group and based on the particular situation. You might simply take care of a minor wound and continue the trip, if that can be done safely. However, you may need to end the tour.

If an injured person can walk, this is the fastest and usually the safest way out. But if the individual is unable to walk, you need to decide to either go for help or carry him or her out. Whether or not to evacuate is a complicated decision based on extent of injury, first-aid skill level of group members, terrain, weather conditions, distance from help, time of day, and number of people in your group.

If evacuation is definitely not possible, part of the group should go for help and the remainder should begin constructing an emergency bivouac. If there are only two people, the non-injured person should leave extra food, water, and gear

BLISTER ON ST. HELENS

A few years back, we decided to go minimalist when climbing Mount St. Helens. We wanted to make the hike to the top as comfortable as possible carrying only a light pack so we would have plenty of energy left to ride down. Without skimping, we split up the essential gear among the six of us, first-aid kit included.

The three-mile hike from Climbers Bivouac to timberline on the Ptarmigan Trail took about an hour. After the hike to timberline, Jennifer felt an early blister forming on her heel. She was breaking in new boots and experiencing some heel lift. The sore spot was red but the blister was not quite formed.

I pulled out the duct tape, Jennifer had the waterproof first-aid tape, Matt handed over the moleskin, and Tim supplied a bit of tissue. We took out the boot liner and padded it with duct tape to smooth out the pressure point. We bandaged the reddened area with moleskin, using the tissue to keep the moleskin from sticking directly to the sore. We put waterproof first-aid tape over the top to seal the bandage. The rest of the climb was tough but successful.

Atop St. Helens, steam hissed and gurgled eerily from the crater and created a fog that encircled the summit. We rode down the lava chutes, leaving white tracks in the ash-covered snow. Jennifer's heel blister did not bother her again.

with the injured person in a shelter and then hike out for help. Leaving your partner alone in the wilderness is a tough choice to have to make, but it may be your only option.

Of course, all injuries and illnesses should be checked by your doctor upon return.

WOUND CARE

Minor wounds are some of the most common to snowboarders. Cut, scrapes, and bruises occur when falling and from hitting trees or rocks. Minor wounds should be cleaned and bandaged to prevent further complications from a possibly debilitating infection.

First, purify water (refer to Chapter Six for greater detail). Then get out your first-aid kit, wash your hands, and put on gloves. Clean the wound with plenty of

Heading up the south side, Mount St. Helens, Washington

purified water. Copious irrigation perhaps plays the most important part in removing dirt and germs. For larger wounds, use up to a quart of water. If you have a small syringe, squirt the water with extra pressure to help dislodge small, deep particles.

After irrigation, scrub the wound gently with an antibacterial cleanser. Then cover with an antibiotic ointment. This will help keep the wound clean, prevent infection, and provide protection.

Finally, cover the wound with a bandage. Butterfly bandages help keep the edges of small cuts together as long as the wound is clean. If you are in doubt, standard bandage strips may be better to use as butterfly bandages can trap infection. Use gauze and first-aid tape for larger wounds.

Add a second layer of dressing if needed. Wrap your primary bandage with an elastic wrap if available. For wounds on hands and feet, use waterproof first-aid tape, which sticks more tightly, especially if your hands and feet get wet from sweat or snow. Semi-porous membrane dressings also work well for hands and feet as they are flexible and adhere well.

After you apply the bandage, check the wound often. Watch for signs of infection, such as redness, heat, pain, pus, and swelling. The bandage should not impede circulation; check fingers and toes for color and temperature on the injured arm or leg. They should always be warm and pink.

Blisters

Blisters are very common to snowboarders. If a blister occurs, follow wound care as above, with some added steps.

Avoid popping the blister. If you pop a blister, you risk getting an infection under the skin. Often the intact blister acts as a natural dressing. If it pops on its own, treat the blister like an open wound with attentive care.

Cover the blister with moleskin or another type of blister bandage. For large blisters on the heel, cut a hole in the moleskin for the blister. Then put a second layer on top. Liquid bandages that go on wet and then dry to a flexible covering work well for open blisters.

Make sure you pad the area well to prevent further friction on the bandaged area. Check your boots for pressure points. Often adding a bit of padding or an insole, or adjusting your liner, eliminates a pressure point. Consider wearing a thicker sock as well.

SPRAINS, STRAINS, AND FRACTURES

Sprains and fractures of the wrist are two of the most common injuries and are caused by falling on outstretched arms. Sometimes shoulder dislocations occur this way. Sprained knees and ankles are common as well. Knees are injured more often when wearing hard boots; ankles are injured more often when wearing soft boots. A fracture of the lower leg, a *boot-top fracture*, is also familiar to snowboarders. *Snowboarder's fracture* is a broken bone in the ankle that occurs most often when falling forward over the nose of the board. It often feels like an ankle sprain.

A minor joint sprain or muscle strain is often difficult to distinguish from a major injury such as a fracture or dislocation. Check for discoloration, swelling, abnormal appearance of the bone, tenderness upon touch, and open wounds, all of which can be signs of serious injury. Obvious deformation suggests a fracture or dislocation. When in doubt, assume the injury is serious.

The initial treatment for sprains, strains, fractures, and dislocations is primarily RICE: rest, ice, compression, elevation. It is best to rest for a few minutes, elevate the injury, apply some snow in a plastic bag, and wrap a compression bandage around the joint. The goal is to minimize swelling. Be careful not to put ice or snow directly on the skin. Anti-inflammatory medication such as ibuprofen or aspirin may help, also.

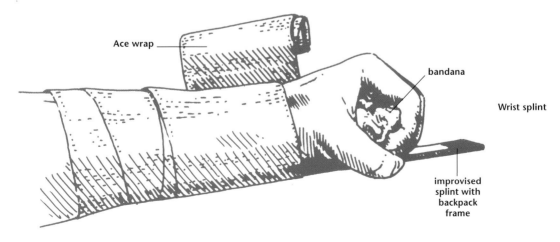

Ace wrap

bandana

Wrist splint

improvised splint with backpack frame

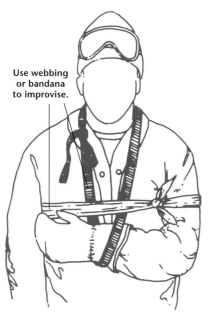

Use webbing
or bandana
to improvise.

Shoulder sling
and swath

After no more than fifteen minutes, re-evaluate the injury. Do not apply a cold pack for an extended time or sit too long, in order to avoid the additional problems of frostbite or hypothermia. In cold, nasty weather you may not want to apply snow at all, as the risk of cold injury increases greatly. For all but minor injuries, you should immobilize the joint with a splint and return to your car.

When applying a splint, span two joints and the injured area. For example, if a wrist is injured, splint the entire forearm, elbow to hand. If the shoulder is injured, splint the entire arm with a sling and swathe. If the knee is injured, splint the entire leg. Ankles are often splinted best by leaving them in the boot.

Use plenty of padding, such as extra clothes or foam sleeping pads. Use a metal splint from your first-aid kit to support the arm or leg. If you lack a splint, improvise with backpack frames, poles, or snowshoes. To wrap the splint to the injured extremity, use duct tape, climbing webbing, extra shoelaces, or what-ever else is available. The splint should be firm enough to immobilize the extremity but not so tight as to be uncomfortable and cut off circulation or sensation.

Always check the toes and fingers routinely to make sure they are getting plenty of circu-lation. Do this by checking the pulse, temperature, and sensation of the fingers and toes of the splinted arm or leg. Loosen or adjust the splint if necessary.

Use webbing
or bandanas
to tie splint.

Leg splint

Improvise with
snowshoes or poles.

COLD INJURY

Early frostbite presents with pain, numbness, redness, and swelling. Sometimes a white patch of ice crystals is evident on exposed skin. With more severe frostbite, the skin looks dull and pale. It is often firm and painless and movement is usually difficult.

As with frostbite, the colder the temperature and the greater the wind chill, the higher the risk of contracting hypothermia. Early symptoms include shivering, cool skin, and feeling cold. Symptoms can progress to lack of coordination, weakness, confusion, and slow speech. Severe hypothermia is marked by cessation of shivering, incoherence, ridged muscles, slow breathing, and extreme incoordination.

With both frostbite and hypothermia, signs are often first noticed by a partner. The sensation of feeling hot or cold and the temperature of the skin are poor gauges in advanced hypothermia. Look for the signs and symptoms noted above.

The treatment for cold injury, including frostbite and hypothermia, is similar to prevention. Warm up, as outlined in Table 3.1. Change into dry clothes, socks, and mittens. Put on extra layers, especially a head covering. Cover all exposed skin. Move around to generate heat. Eat high-calorie, high-energy food and drink fluids, warm if possible. Find shelter. Build a fire, if needed. Get into your tent and sleeping bag.

For frostbite, the best course is to immobilize the arm or foot with a splint and evacuate immediately. Anti-inflammatory pain medicines, such as ibuprofen and aspirin, may help to decrease swelling and pain. If the injured extremity does thaw, do not let it refreeze as this can damage the tissue further.

SUN INJURY

Because of their delayed onsets, sunburn and snow blindness often go unnoticed until too late. As a result of exposure to intense sun and reflection from the snow, pain and redness occur, but hours later.

Minor sunburn is best treated by keeping the skin clean and dry. Moisturizing lotion with aloe may help healing and pain. If the sunburn is bad enough to cause blisters, you should take extra precautions (outlined above in "Wound Care"). If snow blindness occurs, evacuate with help. Blurry vision or, worse, temporary blindness, can debilitate your entire party and you will need assistance getting out.

DEHYDRATION

Dehydration occurs year-round, although it is most common when climbing in the warmer temperatures of spring and summer. Sometimes we are too busy hiking to remember to drink, or drinking is too much work because the water bottle is buried in the pack.

Dehydration often begins with a headache, dizziness, fatigue, nausea, and cramps. Thirst is a late sign of dehydration. Drink fluids regularly and keep your water bottle handy so you do not have to stop and unload your pack to reach it.

Also, poor ventilation can contribute to dehydration. When hiking in the mountains, we tend to bundle up to stay warm. Yet with vigorous exercise, we generate our own heat and sweat. Try to ventilate using zippers and layers of clothing. Avoid overheating and profuse sweating.

Treatment for dehydration is similar to prevention. Drink fluids. A sports drink helps your body rehydrate faster and replaces salt and sugar, as long as it does not have too much sugar or salt. I use powder and mix it half-strength for maximum absorption. Stop and rest in the shade. When you start moving again, do so slowly and watch for reoccurrence of signs.

A good gauge to determine how well you are drinking is your urinary output and color. If you pee every ten minutes and the urine is nearly colorless, you are getting plenty of water. You might even cut back a bit. If you pee infrequently and your urine is scant and dark yellow, you probably are not getting enough fluids.

ACUTE MOUNTAIN SICKNESS

Acute mountain sickness is the name given to a group of symptoms that can occur to anyone, including trained athletes. As noted in Chapter Three, AMS occurs above 8,000 feet. Most people can tolerate lower levels of oxygen with proper adjustments in their route to allow their body to acclimate.

Early symptoms of AMS include difficulty sleeping; headache; swollen hands, feet, and face; decreased urine; general weakness and fatigue; nausea; dizziness; poor appetite; and cough. More advanced symptoms include persistent headache, vomiting, difficulty breathing, shortness of breath, poor coordination, difficulty walking, and impaired concentration and judgment. In severe cases, AMS progresses to life-threatening conditions, such as high altitude pulmonary edema and high altitude cerebral edema.

Treatment begins with good prevention: stay well hydrated, eat regularly, maintain a good pace, and rest frequently. Keep warm and dry. Stay in good physical condition. Follow the ascent guidelines outlined in Chapter Three.

The first step in treatment when symptoms occur is to stop climbing. Rest, eat some food, and drink fluids. Whether symptoms are simply due to exercise and sun exposure is difficult to determine. If symptoms cease after a short break, it is most likely okay to continue climbing cautiously, perhaps at a slower pace.

Symptoms may persist after a rest, food, and water, or they may reoccur when you continue climbing. Treatment at this point is simple: stop climbing and go back down. Returning to the last elevation before the symptoms occurred often resolves the problem quickly. If this is case, spend an extra night at that lower altitude or otherwise alter your route. Ride slopes lower in elevation. If the symptoms resolve, you can continue the ascent the next day. Above all, do not keep climbing if you do not feel well.

In cases of advanced AMS that include signs of impaired concentration and judgment, poor coordination, and difficulty breathing, you should descend immediately. Advanced AMS can be life threatening.

Certain medicines help treat and prevent AMS. These drugs require prescriptions and instruction from your doctor. Consider carrying them if you are planning to spend a prolonged time at high altitudes.

MAJOR TRAUMA

Major injuries are the most problematic because they put the entire group in danger and require extra skill beyond basic first aid. This is why it is so important to seek training in advanced first aid if you wish to spend time in the backcountry. Major injuries fall into three main categories, all of which are potentially life threatening: cardiopulmonary arrest, bleeding, and spinal cord injuries. Cardiopulmonary arrest means the loss of breathing and a pulse and requires CPR. Major bleeding requires pressure, ice, and elevation of the extremities to stop. A head or spinal cord injury requires immediate immobilization to prevent further injury and permanent paralysis. You should learn these advanced treatment techniques by taking a course.

STAY HEALTHY

Remember to stay in good mental and physical condition. Prevention is the best medicine. Treat all injury and illness promptly and seek treatment by your doctor when you return home. And if you don't feel one hundred percent well, don't go. Ride hard, but ride safely.

Following pages: Tushar Mountains, Utah ©James Kay

CHAPTER SIX

INTO THE BACKCOUNTRY

Before you ride, you need to climb. Your planning, packing, approach, and ascent skills are just as important, in terms of safety, as your snowboarding prowess. A steady pace, regular rests, and good hiking technique help you climb efficiently and maximize riding time.

PLAN YOUR TOUR

When you plan your tour you will need to take many variables into account. Planning gets much easier with experience. Assemble all your information, and then plan a route that will be safe, challenging, and fun. In Chapters Three and Four, route planning and avalanche safety planning are briefly discussed; below is a summary of that information, to review what needs to be considered for every trip you plan.

Route

Plan a route favorable for snowboarding. Minimize flat spots, traverses, and frequent up-and-down sections. Keep in mind weather patterns and geographic differences. For example, in winter, the best riding is often on shaded, north-facing slopes. In spring, you need to get up early and ride corn on east- and south-facing slopes before the snow turns to slush. Local topography and weather patterns vary widely. In the United States, for example, the snow and weather in the coastal ranges, such as the Cascades and Sierras, differ vastly from the snow and weather in the Rockies. Your mode of ascent makes a difference, also. If you snowshoe, you may need a different route of ascent than if you are traveling on split boards.

For more detailed route planning, check your maps and guidebook. If you are using a skiing or climbing guidebook, remember that snowboarding an area may be different. You might even hike the terrain in your local area in the summer to get a feel for the lay of the land prior to heading out to snowboard in the winter.

Time

Make sure you have enough time to complete your tour. Avoid hiking back out in the dark. Plan an extra hour or two as a buffer zone in case of equipment failure or an emergency. As your experience increases, you will be better able to gauge your hiking time based on terrain, mileage, and snow conditions. Most guidebooks offer a rough estimate on route times. On a summer dirt trail, carrying a day pack and board, I usually hike two to three miles an hour. In winter I snow-shoe about one to two miles an hour. When climbing steep mountains, I climb about one thousand feet per hour.

Avoid last minute planning and include alterations in your route and extra time in your schedule for sudden weather changes. I plan some alpine climbs a year ahead, and weekend tours at least a month ahead. This does not mean you need to do everything far in advance. But in the summer I obtain maps and read guidebooks on routes I want to follow that winter or spring. In the fall I question rangers and friends at shops who already have done the tour. By the time the first snow hits, I am familiar with the routes and areas I will be heading to that season.

Weather and Avalanche Conditions

As discussed in Chapters Three and Four, watch weather and snow conditions all season, and know the typical patterns for your region. You do not want to be caught in a storm, especially if it is predicted. Traveling far from home takes some extra research and phone calls. The Internet can provide you with up-to-date weather and patterns typical of local areas (see appendix for some weather and avalanche Web sites).

Many backcountry areas have recorded avalanche and mountain weather advisories. Listen to the advisory daily even when not planning a tour in order to become familiar with the snowpack throughout the season. Ski patrol and ski safety officials at winter resorts also know the snowpack well, as they are in it daily.

Reevaluate the conditions constantly—during the drive up, in the parking lot, and during the tour.

Utah's Little Cottonwood Canyon avalanche country

Road Conditions

Unless you live within walking distance of the places you tour, you will need to drive. Make sure the roads are open and plowed, and that you have tire chains stored in your vehicle. It is a good idea to keep survival and rescue equipment in your car as well. I carry a grain scoop for shoveling snow, a tarp, tow strap, sleeping bag, first-aid kit, oil, windshield-washer fluid, flares, and extra food, water, and clothing in my truck all winter.

Access

Make sure the area you plan to hike in is open. You may have to register at a ranger station or ski area for your tour, or even acquire a permit for day use or parking. Park legally and do not block roads or snowplow areas.

Know Your Group

You should know the skill level of everyone you ride with in the backcountry. I usually spend a day or two at resorts with a new partner before heading out to the backcountry. If you are caught in an avalanche, you are relying on your new partner or the other members of your group to save you. Do not put your entire party in danger because you took someone into terrain or snow too difficult for his or her skill level.

If there are snowshoers and split boarders in your group, you may have to break both a snowshoe trail and a skin trail. Parties of skiers and snowboarders work well when the snowboarders are using split boards

Ask

Do not hesitate to ask for information or guidance. Even when I climb and ride in areas I know well, I still ask people who have knowledge of the area about seasonal variances. Call or stop at the local ranger station to get an idea of weather, terrain, and snow conditions. Rangers can often recommend routes. Check with ski safety offices at resorts, or with ski patrollers. Check with locals in mountaineering and snowboard shops.

If you complete a route, offer information to rangers, ski patrollers, or others who may benefit. Always tell someone where you are going and what time you expect to return. Discuss possible alternate routes that may cause you to be late.

PACK

Gear

Do not wait until the last minute to assemble your gear. Some items, such as batteries and film, you can get at the last minute. But a new binding clip or a bulb for your headlamp may take weeks to special order. Spend some time in the summer gathering, checking, and repairing your gear. Make sure your snowboard, bindings, snowshoes, skis, poles, and other equipment are in excellent working order. Especially check binding screws. Remember to include a first-aid kit and field repair kit. Make sure you replace any items used on your last tour.

Get fresh batteries for your beacon, headlamp, and camera. Lithium batteries are more expensive than alkaline, but they last longer and may perform better in the cold. Test everyone's avalanche beacon before each tour. Do this at home or in the parking lot before you start hiking (see Chapter Four). Remember: insisting that your partner's beacon function properly might save your life.

Before I pack, especially for the first tour of the year, I lay out all my gear on my basement floor. I look at every item before stuffing them into my pack in order to avoid forgetting something. I put my clothes in a stuff sack so I do not have to pull everything out of my pack to reach a hat. I use resealable freezer bags for essentials, such as the field repair kit, food, and maps.

Organize your backpack so it is comfortable and gear is easy to reach. Put food, water, hats, gloves, and sunscreen at the top or in side panels. Pack extra, overnight, and emergency gear near the bottom. In general, heavy stuff goes at the bottom and lighter gear, at the front and top. Make sure your pack is balanced; if not full, cinch the compression straps evenly. Make sure you have extra straps. If snowshoeing, you will need to strap on your board when hiking up, and your snowshoes and poles will need to be stowed for descent.

Take extra stuff. Throw in extra clothes, food, and water, even if they stay in the car all day. When you get to the trailhead, conditions may be different from what you expected.

Water

Water is one of the most important things you need in the backcountry. You cannot live too long without it. Depending on exertion level, temperature, elevation, and other factors, your personal fluid needs will vary. Plan on a gallon of water per person per day, more if you are at high elevations, in warm weather, or on extreme terrain. This does not mean that a gallon is what you must have in your pack at all times, but rather, it is a general requirement for a twenty-four-hour period with heavy exercise.

For example, for a short day tour, I drink a quart of water or juice during breakfast and on the drive up. I plan for another two quarts during the tour. When I return to the car, I am ready for another guzzle. Remember to take extra water, more than what you plan on using for that day.

During the tour, I find it is easier to drink water throughout the climb so I keep my bottle handy. If you need to take off your pack every time you want a drink, you will expend a lot of energy. Avoid eating snow as it requires using energy to melt it in your mouth. If you are using a hydration bladder with tubing, know that it can freeze or leak. Be careful if that is your only source of fluid.

Consider using an electrolyte solution common to many sport drinks, as you can absorb water faster with some salt and sugar mixed in. I often mix a powder half the recommended strength with water in one of my bottles before I head out. This also replaces the salt that you lose when you sweat. Full-strength sports drinks can have too much salt and sugar to maximize absorption of water.

Procuring water. Your only source of water in the winter may be snow, and you will need a stove to melt it. Relying on stream or lake water is not wise, as lakes freeze and streams are often buried under snow.

If you procure water in the wilderness, you should purify or at least filter it in most cases; freshly fallen snow is perhaps the one exception. Purifying and filtering can be done by boiling, or using chemicals or a filter/purifier. If you are already melting snow, it is usually easiest to purify by boiling. However, this requires carrying extra fuel beyond what is needed just for melting snow. Water should be boiled for five minutes to kill germs.

The easiest method to purify water is chemical treatment. Iodine tablets are usually included in emergency first-aid kits. Drop these tablets into a bottle of water, and within an hour or so, the water is free from germs. The down side is that the water tastes poorly. Also, consuming too many of these chemicals may be harmful.

A filter is handy if stream water is available. You have a choice of two systems. A basic filter eliminates most germs, including bacteria and *giardia*, a microscopic parasite commonly found in the mountains. Filters alone usually do not totally purify water because viruses are too small to be filtered. A second type, a filter/purifer, uses both a filter and chemicals in combination to purify water. This type of system eliminates all germs. The negative aspect of any filter is that it adds weight to your pack, and can crack or become useless if water freezes in it.

Food

The topic of diet provides fuel for a continuing debate among mountaineers. Some believe that since carbohydrates are the quickest source of energy, they should comprise the bulk of your diet. Others maintain that you need the greater number of calories of a high-fat diet. The important consideration is that you bring plenty of high-calorie food of good quality. Find a combination of fat, protein, and carbohydrate that works for you.

Carbohydrates are easily digestible and should constitute up to 50 percent of your diet when hiking. Complex carbohydrates include bread, bagels, pasta, and vegetables. Simple carbohydrates such as sugar and fruit are rapidly absorbed and give you quick energy. Fat has the highest calories-to-weight ratio, twice as much as carbohydrates and proteins. High-calorie foods include cheese, meats, peanut butter, and nuts.

Eat a good dinner the night before and a large breakfast before heading out on a tour. These meals will last longer than you think; without them, you would be dragging. When on a tour, I avoid big meals. Large amounts of food take a while to digest and cause the familiar tired feeling after eating. Also, eating large meals takes more time during which you will be sitting and getting cold. I find snacking hourly throughout the day without any strict meal regimen keeps me on a good pace.

STAY HEALTHY

Now that you have planned and packed, do not be afraid to alter plans or even call off a trip if snow and weather conditions look dangerous. At any time, turning around and heading home is tough, but sometimes it must be done. Never head out the door if you feel the least bit sick. You should be feeling one hundred percent well before heading into the backcountry, both physically and mentally.

Fording North Fork Squaw Creek on the way to high camp, Three Sisters Wilderness, Oregon

ASCENT

Boot hiking

Boot hiking, or hiking in boots without using snowshoes, split boards, or skis, is the simplest way to climb up. It works for well-worn boot tracks or firm, low-angled snow over short distances. Riders who hike out-of-bounds from ski resorts or take snowcat or helicopter ski trips often do not use extra gear for climbing. However, in soft snow or on steeper slopes, you will probably sink too deep to make this an efficient way to travel, especially if you *posthole*, or sink up to your knees, in soft snow.

Poles

If you are hiking more than a few hundred yards, poles are invaluable in helping you to climb efficiently and to keep your balance. Collapsible poles are easily stowed in your pack for the ride down. Large baskets work better for powder. Self-arrest grips will help in steep sections and on hard snow. If possible, get collapsible poles that convert to an avalanche probe.

When hiking with poles, plant them firmly in the snow and keep pace with your steps. Stay balanced.

Snowshoeing

Snowshoes are versatile and lightweight. They are extremely popular because of their ease of use and reasonable price. Many riders have a set, so most likely you will be able to find more people to tour with if you are snowshoeing. Take them out for a trial hike or two before hiking in the backcountry.

As with poles, when hiking with snowshoes, keep a steady pace and stay balanced. When you step, plant the shoe firmly in the snow and use the entire platform for the best flotation. Try to avoid dragging the snowshoe in the snow between steps.

On steep terrain or hard snow, you may need to place the snowshoe into the snow and push it forward to dig the toe in, a maneuver called *step-kicking*. Apply a little pressure to flatten out a step before you put your entire weight on the snowshoe. On very steep slopes, you may only be able to *toe-point*, or step on the ball of your foot, without using the entire platform.

If you have traction devices attached to the bottom of the snowshoe and the snowpack is relatively firm, you may be able to hike up flat-footed. Again, stay balanced and use your poles.

If the slope is too steep, or the snow too deep to hike directly up in, try traversing using a zig-zag pattern up the slope. This will save energy but add some distance to your route. Turn around on the switchbacks using a *kick turn*. Step around 180 degrees with one snowshoe facing the opposite direction. Then step around with the other shoe to place it alongside the first. This stationary turn allows you to turn around in a small area quickly with only two steps.

Earning some turns, snowshoeing up Mill D North Fork, Big Cottonwood Canyon, Utah

Split Boarding

When using split boards you will need to be proficient at free-heel skiing, at least for ascent. Practice! Most of the time on the flats you will hike with the *kick and glide* step, sliding one foot forward and pushing off with the other. However, with climbing skins on, you cannot glide much. Unlike snowshoeing, you slide your feet between steps without picking up the ski off the snow.

Always plant the split board flat on the slope to use its entire surface area. For steeper slopes, use heel lifts for better leverage. If the slope is too steep or slick to climb directly up, zigzag up, making kick turns on the switchbacks in the same manner as described above for snowshoes.

For short sections of steep slope or icy, firm snow, you may be able to *sidestep,* which is hiking sideways up the slope using the edge of the board. In some cases, it may be more efficient to use the *herringbone step,* hiking forward up the slope with the skis in a V-shaped pattern to use the edges.

Splitboarding above timberline, Cooper Spur, Mount Hood, Oregon

Splitboarding the deep stuff, Big Cottonwood Canyon, Utah

When using split boards, you usually attach adhesive climbing skins to your board. When you apply and remove them, be careful not to drop them in the snow. If the glue ices up or becomes wet, it will not stick to the board. Tape the skins onto your board if the glue becomes wet. Apply extra skin glue after the tour, if needed. You may have the option of installing a tip and tail connecter to your skins, which is another method of keeping skins on if the glue ices.

Summit fog, Mount St. Helens, Washington

Skin wax may improve traction. This is a wax that you rub onto your skins before heading out. Skin wax sometimes helps worn skins grip more tightly. Ski crampons may assist when climbing on steep, firm snow as well.

Oftentimes ascent routes have little sections of downhill slopes. Usually these are too short to warrant converting from ski to snowboard mode. However, use caution when skiing down these short sections. Most split-board bindings are designed for climbing up only. You can hurt yourself or break a board when skiing down.

Skiing

Short skis have been used for a long time by backcountry snowboarders. When using short skis, follow the methods outlined above for split boards. Some techniques such as kick and glide, herringbone step, and kick turns may be easier on short skis. Short skis do not provide as much flotation in deep snow, and may be slower. Also, you will be carrying your board on your backpack, so you will have a heavier load.

Skins that strap on are available for some skis. These eliminate the need for glue as well as the problem of icing.

Crampons

Using crampons for climbing on hard snow and ice requires special instruction beyond the scope of this book. Check one of the mountaineering texts in the appendix.

The key to hiking in crampons is to plant all points firmly into the snow. If you fall, go to your knees or butt while keeping your crampons out of the snow. This will help prevent catching your feet and twisting an ankle, or cartwheeling down the slope.

Your ice ax is your primary tool for stopping a fall. For an ice ax arrest, hold the head of the ax in one hand and the shaft in the other. Dig the ax pick into the snow as deeply as possible. Hold on tight and drag the ax until it stops you. For more on ice ax use when riding, see Chapter Seven.

High up on Irving Glacier, Middle Sister, Oregon

Towing your board

On most tours you will climb with your snowboard snug on your backpack, unless you use a split board. In some circumstances, such as a long open climb on firm snow, it may be easier to tow your board. This can save weight on your back, particularly if you have a heavy overnight pack. In fact, K2 makes a backcountry snowboard with a grommet in the tail for towing.

APPROACH

Pace

Perhaps the most overlooked part of backcountry snowboarding is energy-efficient hiking. The easier you make the climb, the more energy you will have for the ride. Keep a steady pace, or an even level of energy expenditure, when hiking, as with any aerobic sport. Hike too slowly, and you will not make much progress. Hike too fast, and you will tire quickly. On flats or firm snow you will move faster; in steeps or deep snow you will move slower. Your speed should fluctuate throughout the tour as the terrain and snow conditions change. If you traverse steep sections rather than hike straight up, you will save energy but add some distance to your tour.

Your pace will depend on the fitness of everyone in your group. Also, if you are carrying heavy packs or hiking in deep snow or over steep terrain, the pace will be slower. It is important to find a good pace for the whole group and keep it steady.

Heading home in an unexpected storm, Grizzlie Gulch, Utah

Rest at regular intervals to take food and snack breaks; how often depends on your group. If you rest too frequently, you expend energy to restart your pace and may quickly become cold. But do not hike too long without resting. Good communication among group members is important. Do not be afraid to ask the group to slow down or stop if you need to. I find that a quick five- or ten-minute food and water break every forty-five minutes or so is ideal.

When you stop hiking, you cool down fast. Keep a hat and fleece pullover handy and put both on when you stop. Do not wait until you get cold to add an extra layer of clothes.

Breaking Trail

Breaking trail can be the most difficult job of the tour. It is best to change lead every fifteen minutes or so, depending on the difficulty of the route. The leader steps aside and everyone else hikes by without stopping. The leader gets the advantage of resting briefly and then hiking at the back of the pack on a well-broken trail. Everyone else continues the pace without stopping.

When hiking, give people ahead of you plenty of space but at the same time, stick together. Avoid following so closely that you step on the skis or snowshoes of the person in front of you. A good rule is to never let people out of sight or talking distance. Remember good avalanche safety. If you cross a hazardous slope, proceed one at at time. Constantly reevaluate the terrain and snow conditions.

THE FIRST TOUR

I was first lured into the backcountry for the same reason as most other people: the early season anticipation was too strong for me to wait for the lifts to open. One year, when the snow began to fall, Allen and I headed to Snoqualmie Pass. It was raining in Seattle, raining on the route up, and just barely snowing in the parking lot.

We were surprised to find at least twenty other cars in the lot, once filled with people now hiking. We loaded up our packs and started hiking, too. From the outset, we postholed to the ground in the untracked snow. Scant snowcover and heavy, wet snow made for sloppy hiking. We traded leads.

I slowly became soaking wet. Without gaiters, my boots grew wet, also. I unzipped my jacket to ventilate only to find myself becoming even more wet, with snow piling up on my chest as we hiked up a steep section. From the parking lot I had thought it looked so good—we would climb and ride three or four times. After twenty minutes into postholing, I realized we would be making only one trip up.

It took a few hours to reach the top. Once there, we lingered for an hour, ate lunch, and got cold. I had no change of clothes or goggles. When we rode down, soaking wet and shivering, we hit rocks and dirt with every other turn.

But even though that first hike was miserable, I was turned on to the backcountry. I've been heading back ever since.

Stop occasionally and dig quick pits. As covered in Chapter One, follow mountain courtesy when hiking.

Rest Step

The rest step is a method of keeping your pace while resting at the same time without taking long breaks. When climbing long, steep slopes, the rest step can be employed to use energy more efficiently.

When you step onto your uphill foot, straighten your knee and transfer all your weight to that leg. This puts your weight on the bones and allows the muscles to relax somewhat. When you bring the other leg up, pause for a second and take a breath before you step again. This will help you rest and breathe with each step. The idea is to keep pace without frequent stops and starts, which is less efficient and can cause you to cool down.

Ventilate

Another overlooked aspect of hiking is proper ventilation, as noted in Chapter Three. You will generate heat and sweat from hiking, but you will also lose heat in cold weather and get wet when it snows. The key is to balance these opposites to stay both warm and dry.

Use your clothing layers to adjust your body temperature and moisture. If you have pants with side zippers or a jacket with armpit zippers, wear these to ventilate extra heat. Use a headband, hat, neck gaiter, or hood to help regulate your temperature, also. Consider hiking with lightweight gloves and then changing to heavier ones for the ride down.

If you become cold, add layers of insulating clothes; if it begins to snow, put on your parka and hood. Watch your toes and fingers as they can get cold easily. Bring an extra shirt and gloves for the ride down if you sweat a lot.

Sunscreen

Remember to reapply sunscreen throughout the day, as it wears off in a few hours.

SNOW CAMPING

Overnight trips give you access to terrain you cannot reach in a day. Camping in the snow and mountains requires advanced skills, such as setting up tents in snow, building snow shelters, melting snow for food and water, sleeping in cold weather, and preventing your water from freezing. Consult one of the mountaineering books listed in the appendix for full details.

As mentioned in Chapter Three, you will need a warm sleeping bag and a thick ground pad. I use a two-inch foam pad and a sleeping bag rated to minus-twenty degrees for most winter and mountain camping. Use a four-season tent with a rain fly for extra warmth and protection from wind and snow. Bring snow stakes or use hiking poles, snowshoes, or skis to guy the tent. For extra warmth, consider a bivouac sack for outside your bag, or a liner for the inside. Wear warm clothes and a hat to bed.

Set up camp in a safe area. Campers do get buried by avalanches while sleeping in their tents, or walk into a crevasse in the middle of the night.

Bring extra camp clothes, such as thick fleece and down jackets and pants. As soon as you stop snowboarding and hiking, you will cool down fast. Put on dry socks and a hat. Most people put socks and boot liners in their sleeping bags to help them dry overnight. If you leave them out of the bag, they will freeze. You need to put your water bottle in your bag, also. Stow everything else in your pack

Cold winter camping in Mount Olympus Wilderness, Utah

when you sleep. Otherwise the moisture from your breathing will condense on your tent and gear.

Eat a hot meal for dinner and melt water for drinking the next day. Sometimes I cook freeze-dried camping dinners, such as instant pasta or soup, which are quick and easy to prepare. You simply add hot water. Eat a snack or drink a hot beverage before bed to keep you warm all night.

You will need to melt snow so bring extra fuel, at least 0.3 liter per person per day. Use extra foil to insulate your cook pot. Use a foam pad or shovel blade as a stove stand in the snow.

Consider a one-night trip near your car for a shakedown. Snow camping takes lots of practice and patience. If you have a problem in the middle of the night, you should be able to get back to your car quickly on your first trip.

RIDING THE BACKCOUNTRY

Here you go, jumping into the best or worst snow you will ever ride. Big powder rides like a dream—you float through turns. Corn on a sunny spring day is fast and fluid. Yet backcountry terrain and snow conditions are so variable that crud or ice can challenge your skills to the limit. The backcountry is a continuum of snow and terrain. You may well encounter many different conditions on a single day. Here is the scoop on riding the the backcountry.

GENERAL CONCEPTS

Safety

By this point in the book, you have probably read enough about safety. But a common pitfall is to ignore safety guidelines for the ride down. It can be easy to overlook a warning sign with all the anticipation and excitement you have built up about carving up the slopes. When snowboarding in the backcountry, you should continuously evaluate the weather, terrain, and snow conditions. You hiked to the top safely; now you need to get down safely. This is not the time to let down your guard.

Look ahead several turns in advance so you can alter your route to avoid unexpected hazards. Anticipate sudden changes in snow consistency and obstacles, such as trees, hills, cliffs, and flats. Vary your riding style and route depending on how the terrain and snow change.

Be cautious. Ride aggressively but conservatively. Follow the guidelines of avalanche safety. Ride slopes one at a time and keep an eye on your partner. Keep in mind that simply because one rider makes it down does not mean the slope is necessarily safe. Slopes can slide after three or four tracks have already been set. Stop in a safe area outside an avalanche zone.

If you get to the top and determine you cannot ride down safely, retrace your hiking path or find another safe route to hike down. Hiking down is not the easiest way to go, but do not take chances on riding a potentially unstable slope. Also, remember to follow the guidelines for mountain courtesy (see Chapter One).

Early Season

We are all so eager to ride with the first storms in the fall that sometimes we head out before the snow cover is deep enough. On numerous occasions, I have put long scrapes on my board and have bruised my butt on rocks, so anxious was I to make turns. Wait for enough snow to provide a decent cover. This usually means a couple of feet and several storms.

When you do head out, be extra careful of rocks and plants in the early season. Falling on a rock buried a few inches beneath soft snow is quite painful, and a good way to break your wrist or tailbone. Plants poking through snow in the early season are still alive and fragile. Avalanches happen year-round. In the early season it is easy to let your guard down. Stay alert and extra cautious.

120

Riding Resorts

Many of us ride at resorts before they open; this, too, is considered backcountry, as described in Chapter One. Avalanche control is usually not in effect and ski patrollers are not on patrol. Again, it is easy to forget to be cautious since you may be accustomed to riding at the resort when it is open. In fact, many people who hike in resorts in the early season may not be experienced in the backcountry. Anyone can kick a slide down on top of you, so be careful.

The same goes for riding at resorts after they close at the end of the season. At the end of the season the resort snowpack varies widely from that of the backcountry, due to thousands of skiers and snowboarders packing the runs, avalanche control, and other safety alterations on the trails. All your backcountry skills should be in use.

Riding Out of Bounds

Make sure you are prepared for the backcountry even when you buy a lift ticket, catch a lift up, and hike out of bounds. Just because ski patrol opens a backcountry gate and others are heading out does not necessarily mean the backcountry slopes are safe. People have died at resorts, and half of all snowboard deaths due to avalanches in the United States were of riders hiking out of bounds at resorts. Never cross ski area boundaries, closed runs, or backcountry control gates if they are closed.

Remember the distinction between backcountry areas that are technically within the boundaries of resorts and the true backcountry outside resorts (see Chapter One). Ask for clarification from ski patrol or ski safety personnel.

RIDING

Riding with a Pack

In the backcountry, you should always ride with a pack. If you are on a day tour, your pack will be relatively light and compact. Pack it well and make sure everything fits. The key to riding with a pack is to adjust it to a slightly different balance point. Keep your upper body still when riding, and bend your knees as needed to adjust for the heavier load. Keep in mind that if you have snowshoes or short skis strapped on, they may catch on branches when you are in an area of tight trees. Wear a full pack for a few days at a resort to get the hang of it.

Anytime you spend a night in the backcountry, your pack will be significantly heavier. You will have a tent, sleeping bag, pad, stove, fuel, and extra clothes. A large, full pack can be difficult to ride with. It can knock you off balance and you may have to take it off to stand up after a fall. When you use a large pack for a multiday trip, leave your overnight gear at a base camp and lighten the load for the day's hike. Making turns with a lighter pack is much easier.

Fakie

Riding *fakie*, or tail first, is a useful skill that you should learn at the resorts and utilize in the backcountry. It can be used in many situations. For example, if you are in a tight spot and need to ride out to one side without turning around, ride backward. If you are traversing, riding fakie can be useful, as discussed below. With the exception of alpine boards, most snowboards are designed to ride backward with minimal difficulty. If you use steep binding angles and a narrow stance, riding fakie is more difficult.

Falls

Probably by the time you get to this book you will be well versed in falling. While snowboarding, the safest fall is usually a tuck and roll. However, in the backcountry, the tuck and roll is sometimes not advisable. On steep terrain and hard snow you risk the potential of sliding into trees, off cliffs, or into a crevasse—the well-known "slide for life." You will need to use good judgment and decide, sometimes in a split second, what to do.

In deep snow try to tuck and roll once and stop after only one roll. This way it is usually easier to land on your feet. If you fall face down in powder, clear the area around you by swinging your arms. Then spin around so your feet are pointing downhill. You may have a problem standing up, especially in deep snow, as you will not have much leverage. With either your chest or back to the snow, tuck your feet and board up to your butt as close as possible. Then push off the snow to your feet. You may have to mash down the snow before you can get any leverage, or take off your pack to use as a platform to push against. You can also grab the side of your board opposite the slope, which will help you rock up on your board.

On steep terrain, stop immediately. If you tuck and roll, you risk cartwheeling down an entire slope. When you fall, orient your feet downhill immediately and try to arrest your slide. Try to avoid catching the board in the snow, which can also send you cartwheeling. To stop with your feet downhill, lift up the board initially so you do not catch an edge. Use your hands and behind to slow yourself. If you fall on the front of your body, dig in with your knees and hands to stop. In either case, gently and quickly set down your board to slow your slide.

Riding with an Ice Ax

When on steep, dangerous terrain, ride with an ice ax in your dominant hand. This is crucial anytime you have the potential to slide, such as when you are riding on steep, firm snow and a fall would put you at risk of going over a cliff or into a crevasse. Think not only about wiping out, but about what would happen if you were to start sliding.

Riding and arresting a fall with an ice ax takes practice. The pick and spike are sharp—use caution. To arrest a fall, hold the ax head in your dominant hand and the shaft with your other. Dig the pick of the ax into the snow and hold tight while falling. You will get more leverage with your feet downhill and your stomach against the ax. However, if you fall with your back against the snow, you should be able to stop this way as well. You must arrest your slide immediately, because once you gather momentum, you may not be able to stop. Riders that are proficient with an ax dig into the snow reflexively at the same time they fall.

Riding with Poles

You can ride with a collapsed pole with a self-arrest grip in your hand similar to an ice ax. Usually this is not as strong or efficient in stopping a slide as is an ice ax. But if you are going on a short trip, this is a lightweight alternative. I sometimes carry self-arrest grips for my poles in my pack. If I climb a steep, icy section, I can quickly screw the grips on for additional support.

Sometimes, riding with a pole or two is advantageous for other reasons. Poles come in particularly handy when you are riding out a long, snow-covered trail or road that is relatively low-angled or has a few short, flat sections. A few pushes with a pole can boost you right through a flat section of terrain without having to get out of the bindings and walk. For balance on traverses or for getting up in soft snow, poles can be useful as well.

If I ride with a pole, I usually use one collapsible pole in the retracted position with a self-arrest grip handle. The shortened pole and self-arrest grip make the pole easy to carry. You can also ride with one or two poles extended for maximum assistance.

RIDING BACKCOUNTRY TERRAIN

Steeps

Steep slopes are found everywhere in the backcountry, and as you get better at snowboarding, you will gravitate to the challenge of this terrain. The key to riding steep slopes is to stay in control and ride rhythmically. Look ahead and watch for changes or potential hazards on the terrain. Keep your knees bent, your

Early morning spring corn, Mill D North Fork, Big Cottonwood Canyon, Utah

hands out in front of you, and your upper body still. This will give you a quicker response when turning from one edge to another, and keep your center of gravity low for better balance. In chutes, gullies, and couloirs that are narrow and steep, keep your turns tight and controlled.

Make sure your edges are sharp and your boots are snug in the bindings, so as not to lose energy through a loose connection with your board. The need to have excellent edge control is why many snowboard mountaineers like hard boots and plate bindings. Likewise, a shorter, stiffer board, steep binding angles, and a narrow stance allow for quick, tight turns and superior edge control.

When you ride steeps, you often use the *jump turn*, a quick, 180-degree spin turn in the air. When riding or at rest, bend your knees and spring off your board's edge into the air. Once in the air, quickly pivot your board 180 degrees, leading with your upper body. Land on the other edge of your board facing in the other direction. The jump turn requires practice, but is invaluable in steep and narrow spots in which a full turn is not permitted or advisable.

In some cases, you might not be able to even jump turn. In very narrow, steep areas where a turn might risk losing control, *sideslip* by skidding sideways downhill, or traverse.

Jumps and Ollies

In the backcountry, it is sometimes necessary to "catch air," or jump, to negotiate a section of the mountain. Many lips, bumps, and knolls will give you a bit of air. Narrow crevasses, cornices, and rocks might be easier and safer to jump than hike around. Be cautious as cornices can avalanche and you can get hurt from landing the jump, also. Similarly, crevasses and rocks are not always best negotiated by jumping. Jumping is a skill you should practice first at resorts. Start small, then go big.

An *ollie*, also known as a bunny hop, is a short skateboard maneuver, in which you spring off the snow to catch air without the aid of a snow ramp or gravity. An ollie is usually executed on flats or moderately angled slopes to clear small rocks, downed limbs, or other obstacles. Some obstacles can surprise you and you may not be able to suddenly stop. An ollie will help you clear these quickly. Again, practice at resorts first.

When jumping or ollieing, always check your landing first. Have someone not jumping scout the landing spot, or check it out yourself and then hike back up. Make sure the landing is in soft snow, free of obstacles, and steep enough to land and glide. Also, check the exposure beyond the jump in case you fall and slide. As mentioned earlier, it is not only wiping out on a jump that should concern you. If you fall and slide or land out of control, you want to be assured in advance that you will not slide off a cliff or into a tree.

Approach the jump maintaining your balance. Bend your knees when you launch. Keep your body and weight centered and your hands forward. When executing an ollie, spring to get lift. While in the air, stay upright; bend at the knees, not the back. Keep your head up and look at your landing. When you land, keep your knees bent to cushion your body. Land on your entire board, equally on both feet, in riding position. Keep your weight centered or slightly back to stay balanced.

Trees

Treed areas are part of the fun of riding backcountry and often where the best snow lies. When in trees, make sure they are spaced widely enough to ride through them comfortably. Steer toward open areas. Keep your turns tight. An area of trees is not the place in which to make long, carving turns.

Look ahead, wear eye protection, and watch the stuff strapped on your pack. Be prepared to stop and react quickly. Anticipate sudden changes in direction. Do not ride too close to tree wells and avoid riding in terrain traps like gullies and streambeds if there is avalanche potential. Small slides in these natural half-pipes can easily bury you.

Fresh tracks in the secret aspen grove, Big Cottonwood Canyon, Utah

Traverses

If flats are the bane of snowboarders, traverses run a close second. Traversing long sections can be tiring, especially if you are on your toe edge. Consider using a pole to help your balance, as discussed earlier. Learn to ride fakie so you can ride backward on your heel edge, or switch from backside to frontside frequently when traversing.

Glaciers

Glaciers and permanent snowfields constitute an entire segment of mountaineering that requires extra skill in crevasse travel and rescue. In the late spring and summer, many glaciated peaks are accessible for climbing and riding.

You will have to time your climb carefully. Usually, hiking up at night or early morning is best as the cool air keeps the snow and ice frozen. Ride later in the day when the snow has softened, as discussed below.

Many glaciated peaks necessitate being roped to your partner while climbing. This is primarily so that if one person falls into a crevasse, the other can stop the fall and haul out the partner. It is not advisable to snowboard down while roped up. First, it is nearly impossible to synchronize your turns with your partner while on the rope. Second, if one rider falls into a crevasse, it is too difficult for the other to stop the fall. Both riders are likely to be dragged in. Basically, if the slope is dangerous enough to require a rope while ascending or descending, hike down.

RIDING BACKCOUNTRY SNOW

Powder

Snowboarders all dream the white dream of riding effortlessly through light, dry powder. For backcountry snowboarders, powder is at the top of the snow chain.

Powder is ridden differently from most other snow. You will likely want your bindings centered one to two inches back to help keep the nose of your board from diving. Weight your back foot a bit more to keep your tip up but keep your body centered over your stance. You want to avoid the nose *pearling*, or diving down, into the snow.

When turning in powder, you will not use your edges or carve turns. Use the entire surface area of the board to bank against the snow. Sink the tail and keep the tip up. Use the tail to dig in and hold on to turns, while staying balanced on the board. Avoid riding the tail only; use the entire length of your board.

Stay balanced and maintain momentum. On shorter boards and in deep snow, you may need to bounce or spring up and down through turns. This will make it easier to stay afloat and lessen the possibility of dumping speed in your turns. When you have more experience and a bigger board, especially a swallowtail, you will be able to cruise through turns without bouncing.

Whatever your style, keep your speed up to stay on top of the snow and avoid stalling.

Slush

Slush is heavy, wet, dense snow that often occurs with warm, wet storms and in the warm temperatures of spring and summer. For the most part, ride slush like powder. Glide through this soft snow patiently. You will feel more resistance, as if you are moving in slow motion.

Legendary powder, Utah's Wasatch Range

Crud

Crud is a catch-all category that usually denotes dense snow that is uneven in consistency. Crud is usually thick, heavy, wet, chunky, and variable. It may be cut up from other riders, skiers, or snowslides. The important point about crud is to be prepared for nearly any change in the snow's consistency or the terrain. Look for large, untracked patches that might be easier to turn in. Try shaded areas and sunny areas; one might be better than the other. Depending on the time of day, temperature, elevation, and weather, some areas will have better snow.

Bouncing and jump turns may help you negotiate the snow as well. Weighting your back foot may help, as when in powder, but keep your body centered. If the crud is not easy enough to ride, you may need to avoid that area of backcountry until the snow conditions improve.

Crust

Crust is a hard surface on the top of softer snow that is formed by wind, sun, rime, or rain. Crust can be quite hard and will support a snowboard very well. If this is the case, you can ride on the surface. You ride hard, firm crust just like ice, as discussed below. Be prepared to arrest falls quickly. If you slide on hard crust, it may be difficult to stop your fall.

Crust can also be breakable or soft. In this case, depending on how thick it is, you might have to use jump turns to get through the snow.

Corn

Corn is a supportive crust formed by the melt-freeze cycle (discussed in Chapter Four). The snowpack freezes overnight to a firm crust, which makes hiking up easy. Then the spring sun begins to melt the first few inches to soft, kernel-sized balls. Riding this top few inches without breaking the crust yields a fast, fluid ride. In the spring, corn can be excellent riding, often close to powder in thrill. As the day warms, the sun melts deeper into the snowpack, and at some point turns corn to slush.

Spring corn on Monitor Ridge, Mount St. Helens, Washington

To get good corn, get up early and check temperatures to see what areas and elevations froze the night before. The window of opportunity for good corn is often narrow and early on sunny spring days. Later in the spring corn may not freeze overnight, and the snowpack will stay slushy all day and night.

As a courtesy, try to ride corn early and head home before it becomes slush.

Summer firn on Suskdorf Ridge, Mount Adams, Washington

Once the snow becomes slush, you'll leave big ruts in the snowpack and will not be able to ride it as corn the next day.

Firn

Firn is the hard, dense snow that lingers year-round on glaciers and permanent snowfields. Usually firn is widely variable, depending on temperature and other conditions. In the summer, glacier snow usually contains *sun cups,* depressions formed from the sun's heat that range from a few inches to several feet across. If sun cups are small, you can feel the vibrations of your board underfoot. If they are large, you may need to jump turn through them, as when riding moguls. Wind, rain, and varying temperatures can create a variety of textures and densities.

Just like corn, firn will warm and become slushy later in the day. It is best to hike up early, wait for the snow to soften a bit, and then ride down before the firn becomes too soft.

Ice

Ice is difficult and dangerous to climb, more so to ride on. Sometimes a patch surprises you; other times entire slopes are covered with ice. If you hit ice, edge control is vital. Make sure your edges are sharp. Also, your boots and bindings should be snug for maximum control.

When you hit ice, get on and off your edge quickly to avoid chattering. Stay balanced and make smooth, controlled turns. Avoid dramatic movements. Sometimes you will have to slide through your turns. Try to slow down your speed as much as possible to maintain control. Sometimes you can find soft snow or softer ice on the slope edges or in patches, on which to turn. If you fall, arrest yourself immediately.

Outdoor Books by the Experts

Whatever the season, whatever your sport, The Mountaineers Books has the resources for you. Our FREE CATALOG includes over 350 titles on climbing, hiking, mountain biking, paddling, backcountry skiing, snowshoeing, adventure travel, natural history, mountaineering history, and conservation, plus dozens of how-to books to sharpen your outdoor skills.

All of our titles can be found at or ordered through your local bookstore or outdoor store. Just mail in this card or call us at 800·553·4453 for your free catalog. Or send us an e-mail at mbooks@mountaineers.org.

Name_____

Address_____

City_____ State _____ Zip+4 _____ - _____

E-mail_____

578-6

Outdoor Books by the Experts

Whatever the season, whatever your sport, The Mountaineers Books has the resources for you. Our FREE CATALOG includes over 350 titles on climbing, hiking, mountain biking, paddling, backcountry skiing, snowshoeing, adventure travel, natural history, mountaineering history, and conservation, plus dozens of how-to books to sharpen your outdoor skills.

All of our titles can be found at or ordered through your local bookstore or outdoor store. Just mail in this card or call us at 800·553·4453 for your free catalog. Or send us an e-mail at mbooks@mountaineers.org.

Name_____

Address_____

City_____ State _____ Zip+4 _____ - _____

E-mail_____

578-6

NO POSTAGE
NECESSARY
IF MAILED
IN THE
UNITED STATES

BUSINESS REPLY MAIL

FIRST-CLASS MAIL   PERMIT NO. 85063   SEATTLE, WA

POSTAGE WILL BE PAID BY ADDRESSEE

THE MOUNTAINEERS BOOKS
1001 SW KLICKITAT WAY STE 201
SEATTLE WA 98134-9937

NO POSTAGE
NECESSARY
IF MAILED
IN THE
UNITED STATES

BUSINESS REPLY MAIL

FIRST-CLASS MAIL   PERMIT NO. 85063   SEATTLE, WA

POSTAGE WILL BE PAID BY ADDRESSEE

THE MOUNTAINEERS BOOKS
1001 SW KLICKITAT WAY STE 201
SEATTLE WA 98134-9937

RIDE ON

The planning was long and detailed. You made phone calls to rangers and listened to the weather radio daily for a month. You watched the Internet for weather and snow patterns. You studied the maps and read the guidebook so many times that you have the route, elevations, and landmarks memorized. For a month, the basement floor was littered with gear: repair materials, first-aid kit, boots, dehydrated food, camp stove, and fuel. Slowly the mess coalesced into an organized heap and made its way into the pack, in a way that only you know how to get at it.

The day you leave seems hurried with anticipation. You drive late into the night in an unreliable vehicle. Your buddy is behind the wheel while you peer at the road map using your headlamp for light. You camp at the trailhead and awaken the next day to a cold, hard light and blue sky. The midnight blue sky sizzles as you watch the dawn explode. You go about your morning business of making coffee until you turn around and see the big peak staring at you, powerful, dominating. You trace the route on an invisible chalkboard on the mountains and laugh nervously with your friends.

The hike up is long and hard. At first you hike on sand and dirt and rock. The approach trail is smooth. When you reach the first snowfields, you feel the warm air turn cool as you hike across the slush. Your feet become sore and your back aches from the heavy pack.

The second night is spent high on the mountain and you feel pure. The air at 10,000 feet is clean and cold and washes your lungs in purity. You awaken in the middle of the night to a sky filled with more stars than you've ever seen in a thousand city nights. You put on a hat and burrow deep in your sleeping bag.

Morning brings the summit push. It is long and difficult. You feel as if the climb will never end. Finally you crest the last glacial ridge to the summit. You can climb no farther. You have summited. You sit back in the warm sun, eat, drink, take a few photos, laugh, and high-five your friends. Soon enough you will hike out and be back home where duties await. Perhaps you will have a slide show when you return. But now comes what you've been waiting for, what makes the summit so much more worthy: the ride down. The complex mix of emotions—anticipation, fear, thrill, awe, euphoria—cannot be explained easily to those who neither climb nor ride. Sometimes you do not even try.

HEADING HOME

Making the decision to stay or head home can be difficult if you are having an excellent day. But deciding to leave can also be a relief if a storm rolls in or if you are tired. Whatever the case, when it is time to go home, go home. Stick to your plan. Do not try to get one more run in or you may be hiking home in the dark or spending an unexpected night out. If you are tired, you might easily let your guard down and get hurt. Accidents most often occur at the end of the day.

If one person in the group is ready to head back, everyone should. Do not split up your party or risk a tired rider becoming injured. With good judgment, you will have many more days in the backcountry.

You should be just as cautious on the way home with respect to mountain and avalanche safety. Everyone in your group will be tired but the snowpack has possibly changed throughout the day. If you plan well, you may be able to ride all the way back to your car.

Skinning alongside the snowshoe trail, Mount Wolverine, Utah

GLOSSARY

Acute mountain sickness: a collection of symptoms caused by low oxygen levels in the air at high elevations.

Alpine skiing: a fixed-heel style of skiing that most people do at resorts; also called downhill skiing.

Alpine snowboarding: a style of snowboarding that utilizes plate bindings and hard boots, and focuses on carving turns and racing.

Alpine touring: a style of skiing, also called randonée, characterized by bindings with a free heel for climbing that then lock down for skiing.

Altimeter: a barometer that calculates elevation.

Aspect: the direction in which a slope faces.

Avalanche transceiver: also called a beacon, this electronic unit transmits and receives a radio frequency signal for use in avalanche rescue.

Backcountry snowboarding: riding any area outside the boundaries or operating hours of a developed mountain resort.

Backside turn: a turn using the heel-side edge of the snowboard with the rider's back uphill; this turn is counterclockwise for regular-foot riders.

Bivouac: a small, temporary camp or un-scheduled overnight in the mountains necessitated by a storm or other problems; also known as a bivy.

Bivouac sack: a windproof, waterproof overbag for sleeping; used for additional warmth, emergency bivouacs, or as a replacement for a tent on summer tours.

Blue ice: solid, rock-hard ice.

Boot hiking: hiking in boots without snow-shoes, skis, or splitboards.

Boot-top fracture: a broken lower leg bone located at the top of the boot.

Cairn: a short stack of rocks used to mark a trail.

Camber: the curved shape built into a snowboard.

Cap construction: a snowboard manufacturing technique in which all layers are laminated and the top sheet is wrapped around the edge to form the sidewall.

Carabiner: a metal snap link used by mountaineers to attach ropes and webbing to anchors.

Clinometer: a protractor with a plum bob used to measure slope angle.

Cloud cap: clouds that settle around the peak of a mountain.

Compression test: a snow stability test performed in a snow pit by isolating a block of snow and then tapping a shovel placed on top of the block.

Corn: a type of snow formed during the melt-freeze cycle; the first few inches of crust soften to pellet-sized granules.

Cornice: a thick snow outcrop on a ridge, generated by persistent wind.

Crampon: a plate of metal spikes attached to the bottom of a boot for climbing on hard snow and ice.

Crevasse: a fissure or deep cavern in a glacier.

Crud: heavy, dense snow that is uneven in consistency and depth.

Crust: a hard layer of snow that overlies

softer snow; caused by rain, sun, rime, or wind exposure.

Declination: the local variance between magnetic north and true north measured east or west in degrees.

Deep snow immersion: when a rider falls headfirst into deep snow; often causes death by suffocation.

Depth hoar: a buried layer of faceted snow; also called sugar snow.

Directional shape: a snowboard designed with different tip and tail characteristics regarding scoop, flex, and other factors.

Effective edge: the amount of snowboard edge in contact with the snow; usually the overall length adjusted for nose and tail scoop.

Equilibrium form: a type of snow crystal formed with rounding; also called rounded crystals.

Extruded: a snowboard base formed by forcing polymer through a die.

Faceting: a type of snow metamorphosis, also known as recrystallization, that creates weakly bonded faceted crystals, also called kinetic growth form; the resulting snow is often called sugar snow or loud powder.

Fakie: riding tail first.

Field bearing: a compass reading taken from landmarks in the field based on magnetic north.

Firn: compacted, consolidated snow, also called *névé,* formed by repeated melt-freeze cycles and pressure; found year-round on permanent snowfields and glaciers in spring and summer.

Firn skis: short, lightweight skis designed for spring or summer glacier mountaineering.

Flagging: a process in which the uphill or windward branches are removed from a tree due to an avalanche or persistent high winds, respectively.

Flex: the pliability of a snowboard.

Fluke: a snow anchor.

Free riding: a style of riding, also called all-mountain snowboarding, that covers all types of snow conditions and terrain.

Freestyle snowboarding: a style of snowboarding that focuses on aerial maneuvers and tricks.

Frontside turn: a turn that uses the toe-side edge of the snowboard with the rider's chest facing uphill; this turn is clockwise for regular-foot riders.

Frostbite: a skin injury caused by freezing.

Frost nip: a minor skin irritation from the cold.

Giardia: a microscopic parasite found in mountain streams.

Glacier: a large ice flow covering a mountain slope with year-round snow.

Glisse: refers to all edged snow tools, including alpine, telemark, and alpine touring skis, as well as snowboards.

Global positioning system (GPS): an electronic device that determines position in longitude and latitude by using navigational satellites.

Goofy foot: the preference of a few riders to ride with the right foot forward.

Graupel: round, hail-like snow.

Gray ice: an area of extremely hard, compacted snow or soft ice.

Hard boots: stiff plastic boots designed for alpine snowboarding and used with plate bindings.

Herringbone step: hiking forward up a slope with skis in a V-shaped pattern to use the edges.

High altitude cerebral edema: an end-stage condition of acute mountain sickness that occurs when fluid fills the brain.

High altitude pulmonary edema: an end-stage condition of acute mountain sickness that occurs when fluid fills the lungs.

High-back bindings: bindings constructed with two or three straps that buckle over the top of the foot to be used with soft boots; also known as soft bindings.

Hoar frost: a type of crystal that forms from frozen dew on the snow; also called surface hoar.

Hypothermia: an illness caused by lowering of the body's core temperature.

Ice avalanche: a type of avalanche in which ice becomes unstable and collapses.

Ice ax: a tool designed to assist climbing and arrest falls on steep terrain and hard snow.

Ice screw: an ice anchor.

Induction method: an advanced type of avalanche beacon search; also called tangent method.

Islands of safety: large rocks or groups of trees that may provide some protection from avalanches on an otherwise open slope.

Jump turn: a quick turn made by springing off the snow and rotating 180 degrees in the air.

Kick turn: a stationary turn usually performed on a switchback and completed by placing one foot 180 degrees in the opposite direction and following with the other alongside.

Kick and glide: a skiing technique that requires sliding one ski forward, pushing off with the other ski, and gliding between kicks.

Kinetic growth form: a type of snow crystal formed with faceting; also called faceted crystals.

Laminated construction: a snowboard manufacturing technique in which the materials, including the top and bottom sheets, are layered and a separate sidewall makes up the edge.

Latitude: the east-west lines on a map used with longitude to identify position.

Longitude: the north-south lines on a map used with latitude to identify position. Also called meridians.

Loud powder: recrystallized, faceted snow; also called sugar snow.

Magnetic north: the bearing to which all compasses point that is different from true north.

Map bearing: a compass reading taken from a map based on true north.

Melt-freeze cycle: a type of snow metamorphosis caused by the snowpack repeatedly freezing overnight and melting during the day.

National Climbing Classification System: a system for grading difficulty of technical alpine climbs in the United States.

Névé: the well-consolidated snow found year-round on permanent snowfields and glaciers; also called firn.

NNN: new nordic norm, a style of cross-country skiing characterized by a lightweight boot and binding system.

Ollie: springing off the snow to catch air without the aid of a snow ramp or decline.

Pearl: to dive the nose of the board under the snow.

Picket: a snow anchor.

Plate bindings: also called hard bindings, these have a toe clip and heel bail that attach to hard boots.

P-tex: a synthetic base material.

Point-release avalanche: an area of loose snow that releases from a single point and gathers more snow as it slides.

Posthole: to sink in the snow up to the knees when boot hiking.

Prusik: cord knotted to provide friction that is used for ascending another rope.

RECCO: a locating system using a small diode and hand-held microwave unit.

Regular foot: the preference of most riders to ride with the left foot forward.

Rest step: a climbing technique that emphasizes a rest and breath with each step.

Rime: a layer of snow or ice that forms when supercooled water vapor in the air condenses on snow or trees.

Rounding: a type of snow metamorphosis that creates strongly bonded, rounded crystals; also called equilibrium form.

Run out: the area in which an avalanche stops.

Rutscheblock test: a snow stability test performed in a snow pit by isolating a large block of snow, then testing its strength by stepping onto it.

Sastrugi: wind-eroded snow that forms ridges and waves.

Scoop: the degree that a snowboard nose and tail are upturned.

Shakedown: a practice session.

Shovel shear test: a snow stability test performed in a snow pit by isolating a block of snow, then testing its strength by pulling on the block with a shovel blade.

Side cut: the arc in the side of the board measured in radius.

Sideslip: skidding sideways downhill using one edge of the board against the snow.

Sidestep: climbing up or down a slope with both feet sideways for more traction.

Sintered: a snowboard base formed by heating powdered polymers.

Sintering: the process of snow crystals joining to form strong bonds that occurs with rounded crystals.

Ski crampon: a metal plate with spikes that attaches to a ski or split-board binding to provide additional traction when skiing uphill.

Ski cut: a quick traverse at the crest of the slope to check snow stability.

Skins: synthetic strips that glue or strap to the bottom of a ski or split board; hairs or scales on the skins allow the ski to slide up but prevent it from sliding back.

Slab avalanche: a snow avalanche that occurs when a strong, cohesive layer releases from the snowpack and slides on a weaker layer.

Slush: dense, wet snow.

Snow blindness: a sun injury to the eyes causing blurred vision or blindness.

Snow cave: a shelter built into the snowpack.

Snow trench: a one-person shelter built into the snowpack.

Snow pit: a pit dug into the snowpack used for examining layers and evaluating stability.

Snowboard mountaineering: climbing a peak, then riding down on a snowboard.

Snowboarder's fracture: a broken ankle bone that occurs when falling forward over the front of the board.

Snowshoe crampons: spikes or traction devices on the sole of a snowshoe.

Soft boots: a version of pack boots used with high-back bindings that have stiff rubber soles and firm, lace-up uppers.

Split board: a snowboard designed to split into two pieces lengthwise to be used as two independent skis for climbing.

Starting zone: the area where an avalanche begins.

Step-in bindings and boots: a boot and binding system in which a plate mounted in the boot sole mates with a plate mounted on the board; they usually release by moving a lever.

Step kick: digging the toe of your boot or snowshoe into the snow to make a platform on which to step.

Sugar snow: recrystallized, faceted snow occurring on the surface or as a buried layer called depth hoar.

Sun cups: depressions in the snow formed by the sun's heat that range from a few inches to several feet across.

Surface hoar: a type of crystal, also called hoar frost, that forms from frozen dew on the snow.

Swallowtail: a long snowboard with a cutout tail section designed for powder.

Telemark skiing: a style of free-heel skiing characterized by flexible boots, three-pin bindings, and a drop-knee turn.

Terrain traps: small gullies or streambeds in which even a small avalanche could bury a person.

Test slope: a short hill of three or four turns that is ridden to check snow stability.

Tilt board test: a snow stability test performed by scooping snow onto a shovel and tilting it.

Toe point: climbing forward up steep slopes using only the boot toe on the snow instead of the entire sole.

Topographic lines: lines that connect all points of the same elevation on a map; also called contour lines.

Tour: single- or multiple-day outing.

Track: the area an avalanche slides along.

Tree well: the area under a tree where snow does not accumulate as much as on the surrounding terrain.

True north: the direction pointing to the North Pole on which all maps are based.

Verglas: a thin ice layer on rocks.

Wand: a thin bamboo pole topped with a bright flag used for marking trails or crevasses.

Whiteout: thick fog or clouds in which visibility is minimal.

Wind chill: the ambient temperature adjusted for the cooling effects of wind on bare skin.

Yosemite Decimal System: a rating system for difficulty of technical climbs in the United States.

APPENDIX: ADDITIONAL INFORMATION

BOOKS

Armstrong, B.R. and K. Williams. *The Avalanche Book*. Golden, CO: Fulcrum, 1992.

Bennett, S. and S. Downey. *The Complete Snowboarder*. Camden, ME: Ragged Mountain, 1994.

Bezruchka, S. *Altitude Illness: Prevention and Treatment*. Seattle: The Mountaineers Books, 1994.

Brady, M. and L. Torgersen. *Waxing and Care of Skis and Snowboards*. Berkeley: Wilderness Press, 1996.

Carline, J.D., M.J. Lentz and S.C. Macdonald. *Mountaineering First Aid, 4th ed*. Seattle: The Mountaineers Books, 1996.

Daffern, T. *Avalanche Safety for Skiers and Climbers, 2nd ed*. Seattle: Cloudcap, 1992.

Darvill, F.T. *Mountaineering Medicine: A Wilderness Medical Guide, 13th ed*. Berkeley: Wilderness, 1992.

Fredston, J. and D. Fesler. *Snow Sense: A Guide to Evaluating Snow Avalanche Hazard*. Anchorage: Alaska Mountain Safety Center, 1994.

Graydon D. (ed). *Mountaineering: the Freedom of the Hills, 5th ed*. Seattle: The Mountaineers Books, 1992.

Hackett, P.H. *Mountain Sickness: Prevention, Recognition and Treatment*. New York: American Alpine Club, 1980.

Howe, S. *Sick: A Cultural History of Snowboarding*. New York: St. Martins, 1998.

Humes, J. and S. Wagstaff. *Boarderlands: The Snowboarder's Guide to the West Coast*. San Francisco: HarperCollins, 1995.

Moynier, J. *Avalanche Awareness: A Practical Guide to Safe Travel in Avalanche Terrain*. Evergreen, CO: Chockstone, 1993.

O'Bannon, A. *Allen and Mike's Really Cool Backcountry Ski Book: Traveling and Camping Skills for a Winter Environment*. Evergreen, CO: Chockstone, 1996.

Powers P. *NOLS Wilderness Mountaineering*. Mechanicsburg, PA: Stackpole Books, 1993.

Prater, G. *Snowshoeing, 4th. ed*. Seattle: The Mountaineers Books, 1997.

Selters A. *Glacier Travel and Crevasse Rescue*. Seattle: The Mountaineers Books, 1990.

Townsend, C. *Wilderness Skiing and Winter Camping*. Camden, ME: Ragged Mountain, 1994.

Wilkerson, J.A. (ed.) *Medicine for Mountaineering and Other Wilderness Activities, 4th ed*. Seattle: The Mountaineers Books, 1992.

MAGAZINES

Backcountry. Backcountry Publishing, Arvada, CO.
Couloir. Couloir Publications, Truckee, CA.
Snoboard. Railways, Bridgeport, CT.
Snowboard Canada. Toronto, Canada.
Snowboarder. Surfer Publications, Dana Point, CA.
Snowboard Life. Transworld Magazine Corp. Oceanside, CA.
Transworld Snowboarding. Transworld Magazine Corp. Oceanside, CA.

VIDEOS

Avalanche Rescue: Not a Second to Waste. Colorado Avalanche Information Center and
    National Ski Patrol, 1992
Avalanche Rescue Beacons: A Race Against Time. Colorado Avalanche Information Center,
    and People Prod., 1995
Winning the Avalanche Game. Friends of Utah Avalanche Forecast Center, 1993

INTERNET SITES

The Internet can be an overwhelming source of information. You can find useful information if you know what you are looking for and have some experience with the Internet. Any search engine is a good place to start. Almost every snowboard-related magazine, resort, company, and organization has a Web page. The Web sites I have found most useful on a regular basis are those covering weather and avalanche information, as they provide up-to-date information. Below are the home pages; you will need to find more specific weather and avalanche information by region.

Weather
In the United States. Weather Net: *http://cirrus.sprl.umich.edu/wxnet* and National
    Weather Service: *http://www.nws.noaa.gov*
In Canada. Canada Meteorological Center: *http://www.cmc.doe.ca*
In the United Kingdom. National Weather Service: *http://www.meto.govt.uk*
In the world. World Meteorological Association: *http://www.wmo.ch*

Avalanche
In the United States. Westwide Avalanche Network: *http://www.avalanche.org* and
    Cyberspace Snow and Avalanche Center: *http://www.csac.org*
In Canada. Canadian Avalanche Association: *http://www.island.net.com/snow*

Other Resources
Check your local phone book, backcountry snowboard shop, and mountain resort for information including weather and snow reports, road conditions, regional avalanche forecasts, mountaineering clubs, and courses that cover avalanche safety, first aid, CPR, and mountaineering.

INDEX

References to illustrations, photographs, and tables are in italics.

ABOUT THE AUTHOR

Christopher Van Tilburg began snow skiing at age five and snowboarding in 1985. Trained in science writing and medicine, he is a specialist in wilderness medicine and board sports, including snowboarding, skateboarding, surfing, and windsurfing, among others. A member of the Wilderness Medical Society, Chris has lectured frequently on snowboarding and backcountry safety. He writes a column, "Ask Dr. Chris," for *Wind Tracks*, a magazine for which he serves as medical editor, and has contributed to *Back Country, The Climbing Art, Emergency, High Country News, iSki, Physician and Sportsmedicine, Snowboard Life, Sports Guide, Surfing Medicine, Wilderness and Environmental Medicine, Wilderness Medicine Letter, Windsurfing,* and other publications. Chris's home is near Mount Adams in the Columbia River Gorge in Washington State.